What Are the Odds?

What Are the Odds?

a memoir

Ken Cornacchione

Pen & Publish
Saint Louis, Missouri

Published by Pen & Publish, LLC, USA

www.PenandPublish.com
info@PenandPublish.com

Saint Louis, Missouri
(314) 827-6567

Paperback ISBN: 978-1-956897-46-3
e-book ISBN: 978-1-956897-47-0
Library of Congress Control Number: 2024940590

Contents

Preface

In conveying memories from my life's story, I am hopeful that the events, details, and accompanying emotions will afford you a moment to reflect as a kind of conduit to your own life's events. While some of these episodes initially may have created a wide range of pessimistic or even gloomy feelings and reactions, what remains important is how those stories and the memories they created in my life serve as lessons or instructions by which I live.

My targeted audiences are three-fold. First, I want my wife, Cindy, and my son, Damian, to have a clear timeline of my life and the events that shaped who I am and why I think and act the way I do. While they have heard many of these stories, I hope the chronological order and added details will buttress their understanding. The second audience is my grandchildren. As they will receive substantial trust distributions in the future, each may want to know more about who Papi was, what he was like in greater detail, and what made him the way he was. Thirdly, it is my most fervent desire that an unrelated reader may generate a glimmer of hope through a connection to one of my memories or, perhaps, a methodology of how I sought to learn by choosing a different perspective and resultant course of action. I am indeed extremely fortunate.

Parker

Beau at four months

Walker

Memories:
Timeless Treasures of the Heart

I was sitting on the dock on the bay behind my house and marveling at the enchantment water holds for me. The water always seemed to transport me back to a typical summer day many years ago: Billowy clouds like dollops of white cotton candy were suspended in a brilliant blue sky. The crystal-clear water at the lake's edge gently lapped across my tiny feet as I stared down, mesmerized by the darting minnows and the sun's reflections. I momentarily noticed the wrinkled edges of my diaper until the voices nearer the house broke my wonderment. "Boo, where are you? Boo?"

This was my first memory in which I was conscious of my surroundings, of myself and of things outside of my control. Later in life, it would be the things outside of my control that would shatter my focus—and at times my being. Yet, this initial memory also presented an important insight into the moment and was a powerful lesson of free choice. I had choices: to stay in the moment at the water's edge, with its magnetic pull, or to heed a call and return from the water's edge to the calling.

Those choices always ran a gamut, including, though not limited to, staying focused in the moment and enjoying the enchantment that it delivered; accomplishing a task, be it short and direct or longer term and more challenging; or resigning to the distraction at hand and becoming stuck. I would soon learn in the years ahead that there would be times, given my age and corresponding resources, that those interruptions were overpowering and required immediate attention. Yet, I always carried the memory at the water's edge to convey that

I had choices. As I matured, I further learned that those choices had consequences and that those consequences were not always according to my timeline or tantamount to desired outcomes. That choices have consequences and other lessons will follow after a few more memories.

La Mia Famiglia

I was the third of three boys and was born on October 29, 1951. My father, Mateo or Matthew, was born in 1908, which was five years after his parents arrived in America. His father, Antonio Cornacchione, was born in 1885 in Fossalto, Italy, a small town with a population of one thousand or so inhabitants in the region of Molise, located north of Naples and landlocked in the central part of Italy. Antonio and his wife, Margaret Agnes Fierro, arrived in Boston in 1903 via the ship *Nord America*.

My father was of average build: five feet, eight inches or so, medium frame, and around 170 pounds. He had thick black hair which, over time, turned black and gray and thinned; yet his deep brown eyes were always prominent. My father and his parents relocated from Boston to Indianapolis in 1920, at which time my father was twelve years of age. Through incredible focus and hard work, and maybe a desire to escape his somewhat dominating mother and meager background, my father eventually graduated from medical school from Indiana University, served as a lieutenant colonel in the army, and later established a general practice of medicine on the southeast side of Indianapolis, near Eli Lilly and Company and in the center of an Italian American neighborhood. While in military service, my father met my mother, Janice Leta Cross, and they married shortly after the end of World War II. They were married for eleven years and divorced when I was five years old. It was my father who called me Boo and would do so the rest of his life. It was my father, too, though at a two-hour distance from me due to divorce, who would stay in touch, drive distances to attend a few of my high school basketball games, remember my birthday, congratulate me on my accomplishments, and encourage my educational and athletic pursuits.

We called my father's mother, Margaret Agnes, Mamie. Mamie was born in 1889, and she migrated with her husband, Antonio, to America in 1903 as part of the great wave of migration to the United States in the early twentieth century. I never met Antonio, as he passed in his early fifties, during the 1940s, although I did know he was a seamster. My earliest memories, ages three to five, of Mamie stemmed from when my parents were living together in a suburban setting with large acreage on the southeast side of Indianapolis before the I-465 loop was constructed. I recall Mamie being present and not liking my mother because she "drank too much," often said in Italian along with some other choice words which I didn't understand but clearly recognized to be negative from her facial expressions and the tone of her voice. Sometimes Mamie's commentaries would erupt in broken English. Mamie was very proud of her son, my father. Nevertheless, given a matriarchal orientation, she ruled the roost and felt it was my father's first duty to take care of her until her death in 1975 at the age of eighty-six. My father did exactly that.

My mother, Janice Leta Cross, was born in 1922, which translated into a fourteen-year age difference with my father. She was also about five feet, eight inches tall, though with a large frame, large breasts, and thick auburn hair which accentuated her green eyes. My mother attended one year at Michigan University. I suspect her short-term collegiate experience was due to her proclivity for men and alcohol, although World War II had erupted during that time too.

My mother had grown up with an accomplished father, Cecil Cross, who was born in 1895 and who was an insurance company senior executive and former Olympian athlete in track and field. He had studied actuarial sciences at Michigan University and was elected into the Michigan academic/athletic Hall of Fame. I am confident that my fluency in math and proclivity in athletics, in part, stemmed from my grandfather. My contact with this grandfather was extremely limited, as they lived in Fort Wayne, Indiana, and he passed December 23, 1959, at the age of sixty-four, while hosting a Christmas party with his wife. I had moved from Indianapolis to Fort Wayne following my parents' divorce in 1956, my first-grade year of school. Therefore, my exposure to Cecil was sparse in a short period of less than three years.

My maternal grandmother was Leta Harriet Cross, whom my brothers and I called GaGa. She was typically Victorian in demeanor, given her background, the time period, and her age. GaGa was born in 1900; consequently, GaGa always seemed to be at an emotional distance in some respects. During the visits we had, she would always have Archway's Mrs. Linnie's cookies on hand and would typically take me to lunch at Hall's restaurant as I became older. GaGa also always funded whatever school clothes I may have received from second grade through high school; so, in balance, she was somewhat attentive and to a small degree involved. It was interesting to note that my mother always called her father "Daddy" and her mother "Mother" instead of something more affectionate.

My mother also had a younger sister, Aunt Bobbie, who was an incredible person and an accomplished actress and golfer. Early in my life, my aunt and her family lived in the suburbs of Chicago, so I would see her and my four cousins maybe once a year when they came to Fort Wayne to see Cecil and GaGa. In my elementary school days, Aunt Bobbie and her family moved to the West Coast south of San Francisco. In both Chicago and on the West Coast, my aunt had leading roles in major theatrical productions, such as *Auntie Mame* and *Gypsy*. Ultimately, her amateur acting resulted in some national advertising jobs for Weight Watchers, a cruise line, and so forth. Her acting also led to some interesting personal friendships she enjoyed with the likes of Carol Channing, Woody Allen, and others. At the same time, Aunt Bobbie excelled in golf, as evidenced by her winning numerous club championships as well as the Indiana State Amateur Women's Championship, in which I caddied for her. She was truly an exceptional, kind, witty, engaging, and loving person.

My two brothers, Tony and Matt, were respectively four and six years older than I. Before I moved to Fort Wayne at age five, older brother Matt had moved to live with our maternal grandparents, Cecil and GaGa. I suspected in hindsight this was due to my parents' turmoil at home. When I moved to Fort Wayne, I was in elementary school and Matt was in junior high school; therefore, we didn't have that much in common and didn't spend much time together. In the summers during his high school years, Matt lived with my father in Indianapolis and worked at Sealtest Dairy, where he made sherbert ice cream, something he would not eat for the rest of his life.

I believed Matt was more heavily influenced by the initial turmoil at home between my parents and subsequently later with my mother's alcoholism and related antics. Matt was old enough to fully understand what was going on, but he was not mature enough to know that my mother's behavior was not his fault. Both my brothers and I had no knowledge or direction on what to do: We simply did not have sufficient life experience to possess the adequate tools. In any event, I believed those conditions were a cause in Matt, earlier in his adult life, being somewhat introverted around new people. He did obtain his degree in accounting from Indiana University and later became the chief financial officer for the Indianapolis Museum of Art. Matt's employees loved him, and he was a great boss in all respects. His employees warmly called Matt "Nippie," an affectation from his high school days. We remained in touch throughout our lives, although contact was pretty much limited to two, at most three, telephone calls each year on our birthdays and at Christmastime. I always felt that Matt would be there for me at any time and for any reason. I simply would have to say, "Matt, I need you." There just were not the conditions at home in our earlier lives to build a more regular and deeper relationship, and the age difference of six years was significant at the time. Matt fathered two children, Teri and Matt Jr., whom I called Fred and Wilma respectively, and we all had close relationships. Matt Jr. and his wife, Allison, had a beautiful daughter, Elizabeth. Teri had three children: Even, Sarah, and Jacob. Matt Jr. and Teri were always close, and their families were close-knit and full of love and respect. I knew Matt loved me, and he knew I loved him. We shared the same badge of courage: We survived our mother.

The amount of time spent with my other brother, Tony, was limited, too. When I was five, just before leaving Indianapolis, I recalled Tony being spanked with a belt one evening in the bathtub. Tony could not have been more than eight or nine years of age. Soon thereafter, Tony went away for treatment. I believe he had a nervous breakdown. Nevertheless, when I was in elementary and junior high school, Tony and I shared some time together, as he excelled in athletics and I sometimes was allowed to tag along. Most of Tony's friends were athletes like he, and there always seemed to be a need in pickup games for another player, hence my attendance. When I was attending junior high school, Tony was fully engaged in high school and was a recognized and accomplished athlete in basketball and football. Tony had his first serious dating relationship with Karen, whom he ultimately married. Consequently, my time with Tony was limited, though more than with Matt.

As an aside, Tony's life took a dramatic turn his senior year in high school. One December night in 1967, Tony let my dog, Duchess, outside to go to the bathroom. He slipped on the top step, which had a thin layer of ice, and fell. As he fell, his arm went through the glass window portion of the door, and his bicep and ligaments were severed completely, thereby ending any and all future athletic endeavors. It was terrifying, because Tony and I were alone as my mother was out on a date or at a bar. Nevertheless, I called 9-1-1 for an ambulance. I will never forget Tony's determination throughout the rest of his life in accepting the results of that accident and making the most out of it. It was my first clear understanding of one of my life's lessons: **It's not as important what happened, but rather what you did with what happened.** Tony's attitude in recuperation and well beyond were simply astonishing and exemplary. There may have been times when Tony would reflect on what life could have been like if the accident had never occurred, but for the most part, he focused on Karen and, ultimately, his children and career.

Over the years, Tony developed a keen interest in learning all of my father's mother's Italian recipes, or more accurately, he watched how Mamie made things, because recipe cards were not part of her kitchen regimen. Tony's love of cooking carried on in his adult life as a regional manager for Sysco, a food distribution company, in southern Michigan. When calling on new accounts to sell a recently introduced product, Tony would ask for a skillet and use the new product in the preparation of a quick dish, by which he was demonstrating the product's utility while at the same time adroitly building a relationship. I was sure a touch of Mamie was in some of those dishes. Tony loved people, and they loved him. His devotion to his wife and three children was unshakeable, although for a short time, Tony, too, had some issues with alcohol. Tony always treated his family as preeminent from the earliest days of marriage and while raising the children. Tony's family had Duncan, a massive St. Bernard, who was the king of the house and deeply loved by all. It seems as if Matt, Tony, and I all had an affinity for dogs.

Tragedy struck when Tony died prematurely, before his two younger children had even finished college. His passing was unexpected and too early in his life at age fifty-five. Within two years or so of Tony's passing, his wife, Karen, passed from a battle with cancer. In those intervening two years, Karen and I communicated regularly. I was someone who could recall so many details and memories about Tony, and Karen felt comfortable enough to talk about her illness with me rather than, in her mind, troubling her children.

While Tony and Karen's three children, Tony, Jon, and Jenny, were young adults, the blow of losing both parents was horrific and would only be exacerbated soon thereafter by the oldest sibling, Tony Jr., passing a couple of years later. The three of them would regularly get together. I am sure some of this was an informal type of group therapy and support function. I am also confident their love for one another was deep and pure. All three of them were together on Christmas, and I did what I could to make sure their Christmas was special. Eventually, Jenny moved to the East Coast to pursue an assistant professorship at a college while Jon and his family remained in Michigan.

Jennifer and Jon were both married. Jon had children and a wonderful wife, Nicole, and he was devoted to all of them. He worked as a technician in radiology. Jenny achieved her PhD, was a published professor at Wake Forest University, and married Dennis, who also had his PhD. I did not believe Jenny and Dennis intended to have children. Jon and Jenny had solid careers and marriages. I had confidence they had learned ever so painfully that life was fragile and sometimes momentary, let alone challenging. They chose to move forward, for lack of a better term, and I was of the opinion that they were fashioning full and loving lives. I was so proud of them then and continue to admire the lives they have today.

In summary, relative to la mia famiglia, outside of my parent's divorce at my age five, I appeared to be living a normal life. I lived in a middle-income neighborhood; my brothers and I were engaged in school and athletics, and we all had relatively strong social networks with our circles of friends. Most importantly, I had my German shepherd, named Duchess. All seemed at the time fairly typical. As was often the case, appearances were deceiving.

Ken and brothers in their youth

Ken's mother

Ken's father

Elementary, My Dear Watson

In my first five years or so, we lived just south of Indianapolis with some acreage that allowed for a more rural lifestyle which also made for a lonelier existence, with little to no attention from my immediate family except my dog, Duchess. Most of my memories at this time largely stemmed from walking across the acreage through tall, damp grass to our neighbor's house in the mornings, at which time Momma Most would pick me up outside of the entry door to her mudroom and carry me into her kitchen. It was in the warmth of the kitchen where Momma Most introduced me to hot oatmeal and a variety of wonderful, home-baked treats. What I didn't realize at the time was the importance of her *being there* for me and her motherly ways. My mother had been absent physically for a year or more while she had received electrical shock treatments in Michigan; otherwise, I only have a few clear memories of seeing my parents together for those first five years.

There were glimpses of my brothers, but those were generally few and far between, as they were four and six years older and in school. Plus, those recollections were not always pleasant. For example, Tony spent some time in Michigan getting treatment for a nervous break-down. My older brother, Matt, left to live with my mother's parents in Fort Wayne. My father was building his medical practice. I was left alone for the most part, other than my morning rendezvous with Momma Most and my time with Duchess.

Outside of the aforementioned moment at the water's edge and visits to Momma Most, only two other memories from those early years come to mind. One, we had an old, used, wooden milk crate with separations for milk bottles. It was common in those days for the milkman to make deliveries of milk crates filled with sixteen quart-sized bottles to particularly more rural areas, but I discovered the crate conveniently housed baby rabbits. Given the acreage on which our and the neighbor's houses sat, it was common to see rabbits, and rabbits often had babies. The milk crates would house multiple bunnies at once and keep them relatively quiet and in place. Using a baby bottle, I had the pleasure of feeding milk to the bunnies in the discarded milk crates.

Otherwise, the only other available memory is an overheard argument between my parents. I was playing with Duchess in the living room with an army truck that had a missile launcher for plastic-tipped projectiles. I recall also having a toy xylophone and tapping Duchess's head with the xylophone's rubber mallet. For so long, I thought the pointed crown of her head was a result of my tapping there. I really didn't have anyone to ask about that. Anyway, Duchess and I were in the living room, at the end of which was a swinging door to the kitchen, where my father and mother were talking in loud voices. They were shouting and animated. I don't recall the specific words, but I clearly remember the shouting and yelling. Soon thereafter, it was suddenly announced to me I was moving with my mother to a different city, Fort Wayne, where my older brother, Matt, was living with my mother's parents. It seemed so sudden because no one had talked to me about the upcoming divorce, the need to move, why Fort Wayne, and so forth. Of course, I had no control over these events, but I hung tightly to my protector, Duchess, the entire two-and-a-half-hour car ride to the *different city*.

I suspect, as would be typical for most five-year-old children, a move to a new city from a peaceful, more rural setting was fraught with trepidation and angst. It certainly felt that way to me. Plus, there was the condition that I would now be living in a typical 1950s suburban neighborhood, Indian Village, complete with rows of similar houses, myriad neighbors, and what, at first, was an overwhelming number of other children of all ages. The neighborhood elementary school was just north of our house, and the neighborhood swimming pool was just a couple of blocks away to the west. In addition, the junior high school, Kekionga, was a mere two blocks south of our house.

The house was in the geographical center of several buildings for the benefit of children. The setting initially was overwhelming to me and a reason for my diffidence, particularly because my social skills were probably somewhat stunted at that point. While this setting would provide unbounded opportunity and adventure for me in the years to follow, it was initially overwhelming and even unsettling. Yet, I had Duchess as a confidant, companion, and best friend.

Soon after the move, my brother Tony returned from his treatment, and brother Matt arrived from our maternal grandparents. My grandparents helped my mother buy a house and paid my mother's membership to the Fort Wayne Country Club. After all, appearances were important to my mother and her parents. So much changed in so little time. My brothers, given the age difference to me, quickly immersed into their newfound circles of friends and school activities while I was entering formal school for the first time. Indian Village Elementary School would be the launching pad for my first real friends and the juvenile antics that were so exhilarating, adventurous, and joyful to me. It also would be a respite from an increasingly dark and painful existence at home in our new house, complete with country club membership.

The first few years of school were totally new, but the time passed quickly as I swiftly began to develop friendships and became comfortable with the stability of a routine and the boundaries at school. Those days established a pattern whereby I benefitted, for the most part, from exceptional teachers who were adept in teaching and also largely kind and compassionate. There was a group of five or six of us who became regular playground buddies, and, when lucky, I was able to spend some time after school at their homes. Those times were particularly special and valuable to me early on as I saw how normal families acted, how other parents, married couples, interacted, and how normal young boy activities could be so much fun, fulfilling, and in my case, even transporting.

As far as the families of my friends, I observed how siblings could not only help one another, but also joked, tussled, and were readily available as playmates. Those siblings also argued, even skirmished, from time to time. I also realized that some parents established guidelines or boundaries and seemed to be on the same page in terms of parenting philosophy. There were numerous observations of parental directives with correlative child responsiveness. At my house, I was accustomed to manipulation and subterfuge, always conditioned upon the degree to which my mother was intoxicated or medicated. With friends, I was involved in baseball, football, basketball, swimming, and participating in other sports or engaging in mild pranks around the new, larger neighborhood. All of those activities served as an outlet, but more importantly, those activities forged a deeper bonding with the members of our group, and particularly with Ricky. Thankfully, when I was home, I always had Duchess, too.

During this time period, I discovered that God had blessed me with above-average athleticism. For example, I was a pitcher in Little League, grades four to seven, and known for the junk—a baseball term for a pitcher throwing curveballs, sliders, and drop-ball pitches—that I delivered with a fair amount of accuracy and speed. In addition, I was an adept batter. To wit, in one game, with three at bats, I had a grand slam homerun, a two-run homerun, and a single homerun for seven runs batted in (RBIs). There were similar episodes on the golf course and basketball court; hence, junior high school coaches began to pay attention to me early on.

So those first five years of school were marked on the one hand by an increasing bond with a smaller, intimate group of friends complemented with normal activities and outlets. On the other hand, my mother introduced me to a wide range of men, and I experienced the influence of heavy drinking and the unmistakable pain one's stomach emits when hungry. I only recall two times my mother attempted to cook. For example, I remember one Thanksgiving when my mother attempted to make a turkey dinner instead of eating at the country club. She had set the turkey, after cooking, out on the counter to cool. The smell must have been overwhelming to Duchess, because she secretively jumped up on the counter and literally had a feast—only the bones of the carcass remained. Good for Duchess! The only other meal I recalled was my mother's attempt at Swiss steak. What separated my mother's version was that her Swiss steak sat in an inch of oil, not the typical rich gravy. Apparently, she didn't realize that Swiss steak required a kind of gravy in which the meat should simmer and tenderize. For the most part, my brothers and I had to fend for ourselves to eat if food was available in the refrigerator or in the cupboards. Otherwise, there would be an occasional meal at the country club, and we were expected to follow in tow like baby ducklings to our mother.

My only cooking experience in my early life occurred when my mother was out on a drinking binge and I was incredibly hungry. I found a partial package of bacon in the refrigerator and thought I could cook it, since my brothers were out and about, and I had observed the process of cooking bacon before. So, I proceeded to turn on the stove and placed the bacon in the skillet. Apparently, I had turned the temperature setting too high, because as I stood on my tiptoes to observe the bacon, I was greeted with splattering, hot grease in my right eye. I cannot convey the enormity of the pain. A few hours later, my mother returned and said, "Kenny, what did *you* do?" She effectively made me feel bad for trying to feed myself. I was taken to the ophthalmologist, and thankfully there was no permanent damage to my eye, although the pain lingered for a week or so.

The bewilderment and pain of the bacon-cooking episode paled when compared to one fateful day in sixth grade when I came home after school and was simply informed, *after* the fact, that Duchess had been put to sleep. I had not previously experienced death so closely and didn't fully grasp what it meant that Duchess had been "put to sleep." My mother knew how close Duchess and I were; she knew, given the divorce and subsequent move to a new city, that Duchess was my emotional anchor. How in the world did she put Duchess down without any prior conversation with me? My closest friends eventually offered their sympathy and told me that I could play with their dogs anytime, any day. My brothers were fully engaged in their high school activities and friends, and my emptiness was magnified. My mother had her men and bottles and simply told me, "It was time." What in the world did "it was time" mean to a sixth grader who had just lost his best friend and companion who had been there through thick and thin?

I couldn't let go of Duchess not being with me. I took a porcelain statue of a German shepherd to school and placed it on top of my desk. We had the kinds of desks where you could lift the top, and inside was a place to store books, pencils, rulers, and the like. Of course, my friends and I found the inside of the desk to be compelling and competitive arenas in which we could use rulers, erasers, and other materials to create marble rolls. We would drop a marble in the ink-well opening on the top-right corner of the desktop. The marble traversed back and forth down the edges of books and culverts of rulers meticulously placed inside of the desk and eventually dropped through a hole in the bottom right-hand corner. Feeling a marble secretively dropping in our hands was pure delight. There was a certain sense of accomplishment, and of course, we thought the teacher was not aware as we were allegedly so secretive. My closest friends and I argued over bragging rights about who had the best—meaning most complex—marble roll.

One day, while opening my desk's top, my porcelain Duchess fell off and shattered into what seemed a thousand pieces. Uncontrollably, I broke out in tears, and without hesitation, my teacher, Mrs. Bill, immediately asked me to come out into the hallway, closing the classroom door behind us. Mrs. Bill was a large woman who was fascinated with Southwestern and Native American art and culture as well as the Spanish language, and her compassion and sensitivity would leave an indelible mark on me. Mrs. Bill hugged me and gently murmured, "It's okay, Kenny. Cry as much as you need or want. I understand your pain, and I am so sorry." That was an incredible moment in my life and helped me reach a kind of finality and closure over the passing of Duchess. Indeed, **love is the most powerful energy of all**.

She was the same Mrs. Bill whom my best friend, Ricky, targeted when he snipped the satellite cable wires on the school rooftop to prevent the broadcasting of Spanish class via satellite instruction for about two weeks, providing a reprieve from "Qué tal, amigo? Cómo está usted? Muy bien?" every morning, day after day, week after week! She was the same Mrs. Bill who did not add to my embarrassment one day when I returned from lunch and vomited profusely in the hallway. You see, since I didn't always have food at home while my mother was at the country club or God knows where else, I would always eat like a horse at school lunch. Food was plentiful at school. In fact, I oftentimes would eat what my best friends might leave on their plates. On this infamous day, the meal was sauerkraut and hot dogs, and I clearly overindulged. The janitor, Mr. Carpenter, claimed he had never seen anything like this massive, volcanic vomit in his thirty-plus years. The vomit completely blocked all three hallways to classrooms as it was posited squarely in the center. More than once, the story of my vomiting was recalled, likely embellished but thoroughly enjoyed, by my best friend, Ricky, and me.

So, this was the same Mrs. Bill, who had enveloped me in her arms and let me cry as long as I needed or wanted, and always in a soothing voice, telling me she was so sorry for Duchess being gone and that I could always talk to her about anything. Sometime after Duchess's passing, Mrs. Bill further conveyed that I was so fortunate to have had Duchess in my life for the years I did, and I might have another dog someday. Out of my despair manifested this tender gift of Mrs. Bill: a demonstration that there was a choice in how to react, where to focus my thinking, and that **the consequences of choices are more far-reaching than the choices themselves**. I did not intellectually understand this at the time, but it was certainly deeply ingrained in my being and in my mournful heart.

As things turned out, I believe my mother felt guilty about Duchess, or rather simply observed my despair, as I received a second Duchess the summer between sixth and seventh grade. I am unable to convey the joy and love I experienced with the second Duchess. She journeyed with me everywhere I went; I fed, bathed, and cared for her in every way. She was my trustworthy companion, always greeting me after every school day and always available to let me confide, cry, or emote in general. When my mother and brothers were not home, which was more often than not, Duchess was present and always by my side. It is clear why dogs were an important part of my life.

**Ken with Duchess, taking care of baby
bunnies in a used milk crate, from the
Indianapolis Star, November 28, 1954**

Junior Time

In those days, junior high school was comprised of grades seven through nine. Going to junior high school was a big deal to a sixth grader. A seventh grader—having just left being at the top in elementary school—was at the bottom of the totem pole in junior high school. My older brother, Tony, seemed to have blossomed in his middle school years, as evidenced by a wide group of friends as well as involvement and success in *organized* sports. He excelled at football and basketball, and his teams were well regarded in the city by virtue of winning city championships in both sports in his ninth-grade year. As was often the case, I also observed Tony's strong interest and fascination with girls. This was probably normal for his age, but to me, it was simply intriguing. We never talked about things in general, let alone girls. That didn't mean I had no thoughts about girls. I remember walking Susan W. to the Clyde Movie Theater in the seventh grade. Once the lights were turned off, resulting in the seating area being darkened, I put my arm around Susan's shoulder as I was thinking about advancing to the proverbial second base. As it turned out, my arm fell asleep, and no advancements would or even could be made. I laughed about that first date for years. That was the total extent of my romantic escapades up to that point in time. I'm not sure my romantic skills developed much further over those early years.

My group of friends embarked on junior high school, which was a kind of melting pot of kids from other, citywide elementary schools. There were so many new faces and activities, and classes were much more organized and stringent. Athletics were at a much higher level, as this was my first instance of organized school athletics, which meant there were tryouts and not everybody made the team. Of course, in those days, not everyone got a trophy, and I always believed that was the correct formula. Bells signaled the ends of classes and a five- or six-minute passing period to the next class. Lunch was fun because my old gang and I would always eat together and create new antics, like making bread molds in the bookshelves, spreading salad dressing on the bathroom mirrors, and taunting the assistant principal, "Snake Eyes" Cell. Mr. Cell only once made the mistake of bringing five of us into his office at the same time and consequently suffered total embarrassment by our recalcitrance.

Junior high school was a time of extreme growth for me. One, I made many new friends and was able to see how those friends interacted with each other, siblings, parents, and the like. For the most part, those interactions were healthy and expansive. Two, being blessed with athleticism, I excelled in particular at football, basketball, and golf. Sports gave me a playing board on which I could and did achieve. Athletics helped forge entirely different relationships with not only teammates but coaches; and, all in all, I developed a number of well-serving attributes. I learned that, regardless of background or home environment, I could transcend if I put in the work and was focused and persistent. Accolades I received from athletics at this time resulted not only in some self-confidence but also a greater understanding that **actions, far more than words, had consequences**. I learned that some consequences were more immediate, and some were deferred but still traceable. Yet, I sensed that I could control my station in life based on my *actions*. **If it were to be, it was up to me.**

My core group of friends from the elementary school days still spent time together, although free time became a precious commodity as I applied myself in academics, which I found to be an escape from home life and also a means to shine among my friends. None of those close friends from elementary school were on the basketball, football, or golf teams. It seemed during those years, at the end of elementary school and start of junior high, friend time was equated to being mischievous and adventuresome. We were, in fact, vandals at some level. Our intentions were never malicious, but our pranks were certainly outside the norm.

The planning and organization in our escapades were really impressive for our ages. The examples are too numerous to recall, but a few are illustrative. On one of our neighborhood streets, there was a small hill rising from the street up to a church. In the winter, at the top of the hill, we would manufacture snowballs equal to the size of a base for a large snowman. We packed snow on the lower side of the snowballs to keep them from rolling all the way down the hill to the street. We lightly dampened the snowballs with water in the bitter cold of winter to add an ice layer to them. When our arsenal was complete, two of us would remove the wedge of snow, which would allow them to roll slowly, and we would gently guide them down the hill onto the street. We would stagger the snowballs like a minefield so that cars would have to stop and slowly maneuver around one snowball to the next. Prior to setting the minefield of snowballs, we would have prepared a large quantity of regular-sized snowballs as a kind of ammunition depot.

Our planning discussions entailed who was going to make the large snowballs, who was going to wet them down, who was making the ammunition depot of smaller snowballs, and the path of our escape route if needed. This was an early example of a life lesson: **Organization is powerful**. There was a shallow trough separating the base of the hill from the road, and we laid low in the ditch waiting for a car to arrive, stop, and maybe test budging one of the ice balls with the front of the car. In this case, we would pelt the car with snowballs. On the other hand, sometimes the driver exited the car to more closely inspect the large ice balls. Exiting the car was a major mistake, as three or four of us would arise from the ditch and bombard the driver with snowballs. For some reason, we would squeal like pigs with delight: probably a combination of joy in our plan working and the success of anticipating the driver's reaction, which allowed us to deliver a good bombardment. If the driver pursued us, we had already scoped out our escape path—normally through a small opening in the hedges, which led us, a hundred yards or so later, into a dark cemetery. The cemetery had no lights and, at best, a rustic gravel road. No car, let alone an adult person, would venture into the cemetery on a dim, late, winter afternoon—but we would! If the driver did not pursue us on foot, we were just as happy to pelt the car with snowballs. We giggled louder and louder as we heard the snowballs blast into the sides of the car.

Being enterprising young boys, we developed a less complicated technique of being able to lift the thin top layer of ice from the surface of a fresh snow, thereby securing a resemblance to an ice Frisbee, if you will. Those ice Frisbees made the loudest sound when flung toward metal awnings, which were popular in those days in our neighborhood. I can't describe the enormity of the sound caused by a small disc of ice hitting the metal awning, nor convey the sheer joy and laughter so derived.

But what could we do in the nonwinter months? We caught garden snakes and put them in the swimming pools of a few private homes in the neighborhood and listened to people react when a snake swam by. We took full advantage of the blessings of crab apple trees, which provided an unlimited arsenal for our slingshots. We also put smoke bombs down the mailbox slits that dropped into the interiors of houses. One of our favorite activities involved igniting paper bags filled with dog manure on a front porch. We rang the doorbell and ran just far enough out of reach but close enough to observe the house owner stomping on the lit bag to put out the flame. The escapades were endless; but somehow, we took extreme pride in, one, never getting caught, and two, never squealing on the other members of the group. We simply embraced a kind of demented Three Musketeers' code of ethics: All for one and one for all. Of course, had one of us been caught, we had a plan: give the name of *Butch Lapp*, another young boy who lived in the neighborhood! As bad as all of this may sound, it was a complete departure from what was happening inside my house with my mother, and we never harmed another person nor permanently damaged property.

This was a core group of friends with whom we all shared reciprocity, excitement, joy, and a kind of brotherhood. Two of these friends bear expansion. In particular, my relationship with Ricky was and remains special. He was involved in virtually all of the pranks, played Little League with me, invited me to his house for lunch when I was young, was present through my divorce years later, and was there for me any day at any time. This friendship has lasted in depth and without qualification my whole life. While we shared so many characteristics, we also had our differences. Yet, Ricky was a brother of another mother, and I have been blessed to have him in my life. Note that Ricky became a vastly successful entrepreneur and a devoted Christian. For decades, he volunteered his time working in the inner cities of Fort Wayne and Sarasota, contributed literally millions of dollars to charities, and acted as a Big Brother to so many young boys and men for decades. All of those activities remained in place over many years. It is so rare to have had such a good friend for more than seventy years. During all the days and years together, Ricky called me Kenny; and I called him Ricky.

In addition, while I didn't spend as much time with Steve, he, too, was exceptional. He would have me over to swim at his house and to play board games and the like. In our youth, Steve and I traded a passcode: "Do you feel lucky?" That was a signal to enter the cabana in his backyard, open a floorboard, and retrieve a Lucky Strike cigarette to smoke. Those were the same Lucky Strikes that, when lit and placed over the fuse of an M-80 firework, allowed us time to run and then watch the explosion from a distance. When Steve was a freshman in college, he was caught with another friend for burning down the ROTC building at DePauw University. Keep in mind this was during the height of the Vietnam protest days. Steve eventually became the personal assistant to the Maharishi Yogi in Switzerland and then later developed a large financial planning practice in Boca Raton, Florida, along with a statewide radio show. After he sold his practice, he became the second-largest franchise owner of Jiffy Lubes in the United States. Steve always had creativity, far above average intelligence and ambition, and characteristics of trustworthiness and kindness.

One additional friendship is worthy of digression. Early in my financial services career, "the Cowboy," a father figure in my life, referred me to his employer, Jerry Closser. Cowboy described Jerry as a "riverboat gambler with a plan." Jerry owned Zipp Express, which had fundamentally started through his earlier experiences of operating a courier service in the local community.

Jerry developed Zipp Express into a large, transnational, long-haul trucking firm, complete with well over one hundred employees and a fleet of seventy-five or more tractors. Zipp had terminals in other parts of the country, most notably in Laredo, Texas. Zipp moved a fair amount of cargo into and out of Mexico as well as many destinations throughout the United States for well-known companies like IBM, Xerox, and others. Jerry eventually sold Zipp Express for more than $18 million.

Subsequently, he started a commercial construction company, Millennium Contractors, and eventually added two more companies to that conglomerate. Jerry paid for Cindy and my rehearsal dinner, and he gave my son, Damian, a job in the summer. Jerry was always a tough but fair employer. He expected employees to go through a wall for him because he did that and more for them. His business acumen was unchallenged, as noticed by Ernst & Young naming him Entrepreneur of the Year for Indiana. Even more remarkable to me was the degree of involvement and love he displayed consistently and over many years as a father and grandfather.

Even in our seventies, Ricky and Steve occupy second homes on Siesta Key, Florida, for six months of the year, and I live just a few miles south of there, in Osprey. Yes, we often reminisce about our antics and giggle like little kids when we get together. When they first heard these stories, our wives couldn't help laughing, but they also shook their heads in some level of disbelief. In our youth and during the vandalism days, we were never malicious. I'd like to think we had unbridled energy and no lack of creativity!

Additionally, Jerry owns a second home one hour south of Osprey. **Relationships do matter.** I always believed that a true friend was indeed a gift you gave yourself. Those few friendships necessitated attention and nurturing; but without question, those friendships provide me with unlimited joy, trust, respect, and love.

Back to school. During junior high school I would visit my father on weekends, depending on my sports' schedules, and occasionally would be joined by my two older brothers. The typical routine was that we three boys would accompany my father, a family doctor, on house calls and/or to St. Vincent Hospital, where I was born. They didn't practice medicine like that for long, but my father was available seven days a week, and his phone at home would often ring in the evenings. Most of his patients could not speak English and were largely Western European immigrants, particularly of Italian ethnicity. He was often paid with fresh produce, bread and other baked goods, imported cheese wheels, and so forth. After the last house call on Saturday mornings, we would stop at a Jewish delicatessen, Shapiro's, and pick up a bag full of corned beef sandwiches on Regen's homemade rye bread, the type of sandwich which had so much thinly sliced meat you could hardly get your mouth around it. Of course, some kosher pickles were added to the mix. This was our stash as we left the south side of Indianapolis on our way to Bloomington, Indiana, where we watched an Indiana University football game.

Even though we knew in advance that Indiana most likely would lose the game, the adventure was so special. Of course, to a guy who rarely had enough food to eat, the smell of those corned beef sandwiches was so overwhelming that we would barely be five miles out of town before I grabbed my sandwich, quickly unwrapped it, and devoured it in the back seat. After arriving at Memorial Stadium in Bloomington and before the game, I would usually receive my routine immunizations from my father in the parking lot. After the game, we would drive back to Indianapolis and arrive at the Athenæum, an old, highly traditional German restaurant complete with live palm trees in containers inside, black-and-white tile floors, waiters in white dinner jackets with black bow ties, linen tablecloths, etc. We always had the same waiter, Brownie, who, with a wide smile and pearly whites, dressed in a white dinner jacket, black pants, and a black bow tie, always greeted us with, "Dr. C. and boys, did I.U. win today? Well, that's okay, let's get you some good, hot food." I know my father took care of Brownie in terms of waiter tips and free medical care, but that relationship reinforced in me to **treat people kindly and to pay forward what you can**. Brownie knew in advance that I was going to order either rouladen or schnitzel. Regardless, a healthy side of German potato salad and braised cabbage completed my personal feast. I always knew when I visited my father, my grandmother, Mamie, and Brownie would make sure I had a full stomach.

On another visit by myself to see my father, I recall going to an Indianapolis Indians baseball game. The Indians were a Triple-A baseball team and the feeder team to the major league Cincinnati Reds. After that afternoon game, my father took me to a patient's restaurant for a steak dinner. The biggest surprise of the night occurred when the owner, Mike Tamer, approached our table with another of his patrons and friend to meet my father and me. It was Danny Thomas, the famous actor, comedian, and founder of St. Jude Children's Research Hospital. Danny was gracious, engaging, and unassuming. Beyond the mission of St. Jude's Hospital, their protocol that there was zero cost for patients and their families during treatment is a reason that organization is a charitable beneficiary of my trust. This was also another example of how my father supported and encouraged my endeavors and treated others with respect and kindness.

The most important aspect of these visits, of course, was that I was able to get to know my father more meaningfully and to see him practice medicine. In fact, I was his substitute nurse in the summer for two weeks when the real nurse of forty years, Velma, went on vacation. He was an excellent physician and deeply loved by his patients, who called him "Dr. C." More importantly, my father was a giving man and a kind man. His commitments were genuine and deep. He never took advantage of anyone at any time. I wasn't alone in my observations. At his funeral service, there were lines of people waiting to pay their respects for blocks outside the church, which was filled to capacity. While I may not have spent the typical amount of time with my father, his influence and example penetrated me deeply and forever. I fully understood how **one's actions, not words, are the true measurement of a man's character**. My father had outstanding, exemplary character.

As an aside, it was interesting to note that my mother never attended any of my Little League, basketball, or football games. On the other hand, my father purchased a Rawlings catcher's glove and regular baseball mitt for me during Little League years. During one visit to Indianapolis, I recall practicing pitching with my father, who role-played being the catcher. Keep in mind that I was probably eleven years of age, and my father was fifty-four years old. I remember in particular throwing one pitch to him. That pitch was high above his crouched target, and the ball sailed through a panel of his garage door glass. His remarks were immediate and comforting: "Don't worry, Boo. It's just a pane of glass, and it can be fixed. Now show me what you got." How my father handled that event was a microcosm of his overall interactions with me.

Inside school, a number of parallels unfolded. With basketball and football, there was another core group of friends working on a common goal, relying on one another, and the incontrovertible lessons of life learned through organized sports. Those lessons included the joy of victory, the agony of defeat, and the lesson that **things are not always fair**, let alone controllable. There were **always choices** in how I reacted, and all **choices have consequences**. On an individual basis, my competitive nature, focused intensity, and athletic accomplishments caught the eyes of the high school coaches in football, basketball, and golf, as each made a point to meet me. This only reinforced that I had choices, that choices had consequences, and a belief that I could fashion a future more supportive and nurturing than what existed at home. **If it were to be, it was up to me.**

I also excelled and enjoyed the academics of school. Literature was a genuine escape for me, and I was fortunate to have had outstanding English teachers. The same was true with math. My English teacher devised a game whereby if a student spoke incorrectly in a grammatical sense and any other student pointed it out silently with a quick hand in the air, the offending student had to donate a nickel to *the jar*. At the end of each six-week grading period, the teacher used the accumulated collections in the jar to provide chocolate milk and donuts to the class. That methodology was a great teaching technique to reinforce so many things.

Junior high school times were indeed uplifting, expanding, and fulfilling outside of my home. I was learning valuable life lessons, maturing, and beginning to understand there were infinite choices and actions had consequences. Perhaps most importantly, I began to grasp that I had unlimited potential and could fashion my life, true to myself.

Senior Moments

In high school I formed a particularly close relationship with my math teacher, Dick Sage, who was chairman of the math department and in his middle thirties. Beyond developing a certain expertise and fluidity in math, which benefitted me greatly throughout the rest of my life, Dick would invite me over to his house, where he taught me how to play cribbage. Dick had served in the navy and was a wonderful man. Dick's love for his wife, Caroline, an interior designer, was obvious. Both Dick and Caroline adored their daughter, Cammie. I recall Cammie's excitement in getting her first dog, a Norwegian elkhound, whom she named Shasta ("she has to" do this, "she has to" do that, hence "Shasta"). Of course, I knew the love and joy of a canine companion, and I loved watching Cammie take responsibility for and interacting with her new friend. I was always totally relaxed, engaged, and joyful when I had the opportunity to visit with Dick. He showed me a whole new vista of possibilities beyond a genuine love of and somewhat of an expertise in math. He was a gentle man, a bright man, and a loving husband, father, and friend/mentor to me. As the saying goes, the clay was molded during these years in particular, and that bedrock served as a platform that would be built upon to a greater level later in my life.

During high school, I experienced my first deep romance. As a senior, I dated a sophomore, Lori. Of course, I enjoyed her company; furthermore, I relished her family life with two older brothers, a sister, and parents who seemed normal and supportive of one another. Lori and I enjoyed many times together, particularly at her parents' lake house in northeastern Indiana, where I learned how to ski, slalom, and even barefoot ski thanks to Lori's older brother, Phil, who was a classmate of mine. Yes, there was senior prom, and Lori attended my high school basketball games. In general terms, we spent most of our free time together, even with Duchess sometimes as a sidekick in the car. Duchess, as with all of my dogs, was very social, kind, and well behaved. In short, in those days, I repaired some of my trust with a woman and felt I could count on Lori. She was my first love.

About every three months or so, I would go to Indianapolis to see my father, who was still living with his mother, Mamie. In early high school, I would hitchhike, but my father demanded I not do that anymore, and he would forward bus tickets to me. I found the travels on the Greyhound bus to be circus-like. There were occasionally drunks on the bus and a wide assortment of beings like aspiring professional wrestlers. The bus stopped in a variety of small towns along the way, so I indirectly saw parts of Indiana I otherwise would not have and learned some of the joys as well as challenges of traveling.

My father purchased a forest-green Camaro with a manual transmission for me as a high school graduation gift in 1969. He knew how important transportation was for me. The Camaro allowed me to drive to and from the baseball diamond rather than riding my small Honda motorcycle which, while efficient, was dangerous in and of itself. Besides being really cool, the Camaro was much safer to drive in the rain or in the winter with snow and ice. Additionally, the car allowed me to travel to see my father three hours away on some weekends rather than hitchhiking or taking a bus with its multitude of stops, and soon thereafter to return home from college on weekends to see Lori. Parking the car was much safer and more secure than the small motorcycle to which I had become accustomed. The small motorcycle had been the only transportation I could afford, and I could legally drive a motorcycle at age fifteen, before I qualified for a *real* driver's license.

I worked in the summers as a manager of a baseball program for young boys who did not graduate or qualify for organized baseball beyond Little League. Wildcat Baseball was totally funded by the generosity of a wealthy Fort Wayne businessman, Mr. McMillan. I often wondered if Mr. McMillan hadn't made the *organized* team as a youth, hence this particular generosity. I'll never forget one player,

Joey, who had his right arm amputated at the elbow. The amputation did not stop Joey from becoming an all-star pitcher and all-around excellent player. I never forgot watching Joey. He never made excuses and simply strove to achieve his best in spite of what others perceived as handicaps. I'm confident I learned more from Joey than he did from me. In fact, another life lesson was implanted in me by athletics in general and by Joey in particular: **Don't judge a book by its cover.**

I saved all the money I earned while working in the baseball program. My propensity for frugality was ingrained at an early age, and in my junior year of high school, I moved out of my mother's house to escape her alcoholic craziness by renting a room in a boarding house in downtown Fort Wayne. The arrangements required that I shared a bathroom with a long-haul truck driver, and my kitchen consisted of a single hot plate in my room on top of a dresser. Circumstances generated creativity in cooking with the limitation of a single hot plate, but it was simple and quick to warm a can of Dinty Moore beef stew and the like.

Moving out of my mother's house was a purely instinctive action for my own well-being, even survival. During high school, weekends were often filled with my mother entertaining men, profuse drinking and, of course, no food unless there happened to be something in the refrigerator by accident. I always reflexed when I heard "Volare," one of my mother's favorite songs, which she always played while entertaining men.

During the early fall of my sophomore year in high school, I came home after school with two friends, and I was feeling so proud that I had made the *varsity*—not the *junior* varsity—basketball team, which was ranked number one in the state. When my friends and I opened the door, we were greeted by the sight of my mother sprawled out naked, passed out, with some guy I had never seen before. I was so embarrassed and horrified. I convey these events to illustrate concisely what life was like for me at home alone with my mother and to elucidate the absolute need to move into the boarding house downtown.

I had very little money from working in the baseball program, but I was a saver and planner by nature. Renting a room and sharing a bathroom was the cheapest alternative for me. The room afforded me some peace of mind, some quiet to study, when need be, and to generally find some emotional and psychological safety.

Regarding the specific incidents of my mother, I never blamed her, but for years, I sought explanations through honest conversation. Later in my life, I attempted to identify how those kinds of events helped shape my personality and character, for which I was grateful. Let it suffice to say: At that point, I was able to compartmentalize and to take immediate action. All of my life, I believed in doing things correctly and immediately, even if those actions were difficult.

I often reflect on two other noteworthy events of those senior high school days. During my junior year at basketball practice one day in early November, I was inadvertently elbowed while battling for a rebound, and the coach told me to go into the locker room to stop my nose bleeding and to return to practice when the bleeding stopped. I never returned to practice, as I passed out on a locker room bench. Subsequently, I went to Indianapolis, where my father had a variety of medical specialist friends evaluate me. The diagnosis, perhaps unrelated to the bleeding nose and passing out, was malnourishment! Imagine having a mother who often frequented the country club, a father who was the executive vice president of the largest insurance company in the state, and you're malnourished. This diagnosis, coupled with finding my mother naked and sprawled out with some strange man in front of two of my friends, was the crowning event and motivation for moving out of my mother's house. Those experiences forced corrective action and creativity. I couldn't control what my mother was doing or not doing. The only viable choice was to try to find living arrangements somewhere else. I needed to take action. **If it were to be, it was up to me.**

I was going to be alone on Christmas, so I had decided to splurge Christmas Eve on a dinner. I went to a restaurant that was open in downtown Fort Wayne and ordered shrimp scampi. It was a challenge because the price tag of $8.99 would have purchased many cans of Dinty Moore stew and the like. The shrimp scampi arrived, and I eagerly took the first bite. It was my first experience with spoiled seafood, something we have all likely experienced. I complained to the waiter, who blew me off as some innocuous kid. I departed the restaurant hungrier than when I arrived and with less cash.

My first response was to wonder what I had done wrong. That tendency persisted throughout my life. When there was a tremor in my universe, I always thought first, "What did I do? What could I have done?" I developed this innate belief that I could fix anything: It just required more work and/or more thought on my part. I could fix it. I don't know if my background embedded this kind of triggered response or if I was somehow wired that way. It largely served me well, yet situations that would occur later in my life further refined my thinking that I was not always to blame, and that I could not always fix something through more work or more ingenuity. The flip side, though, was my willingness to acknowledge and to accept responsibility when apropos.

At the conclusion of my senior year in high school, Doug, a friend from the first days at Indian Village Elementary School, and I took his father's new 1969 station wagon for a spring break trip to Florida. When we were traveling through the bypass around Cincinnati at 3:24 in the morning, a drunk driver ran us off the road at seventy miles per hour, and we crashed head-first into the cement buttress of a light pole. Doug was sleeping in the back, and the impact knocked him unconscious for about ten to fifteen minutes. At that time, I noticed blood squirting out of my face, a mutilated right hand which had gone through the windshield, causing four broken fingers and severe lacerations, as well as two broken legs. During these instant observations, I suddenly realized that the car was surrounded by four or five local residents who were taunting me with phrases like, "Get out of the car, honky."

Doug regained consciousness, exited the rear of the station wagon, and prevented the bystanders from looting what little luggage we had. The police arrived and called an ambulance, and I was transported to Cincinnati General Hospital, where I lay on a gurney literally for hours in the hallway without treatment, pain medication, or the like. After an hour or so after my initial, cursory evaluation, Doug came to me in the hallway, assured me he was fine, and informed me he wouldn't leave my side until I was being treated.

After three to four hours, I was taken into an operating room where my face was bandaged to the extent that I could not see what was occurring. A doctor was suturing my face. I never forgot the doctor's voice saying, "Lower your right hand." I had kept my right hand vertically in the air instinctively to reduce the blood flow. Suddenly, two people grabbed me near the wrist and elbow to immobilize my arm, which they lowered, and the doctor began to swab my broken fingers and lacerations with an antiseptic solution. I screamed in pain and jerked my head away from the suturing process. Among other occurrences, I never understood the absence of sufficient pain medication. In any event, I heard the operating door burst open and recognized my father's voice: "I'm his father, and I'm a doctor. What is going on in here?" Within the hour, I received appropriate pain medication, was superficially bandaged, had splints positioned on both legs and arms, and was placed in the back of my father's car for an exhilarating, one-hundred-miles-per-hour ride back to Indianapolis and St. Vincent Hospital, where my father's specialist friends treated me. Serendipitously, I was placed in the same hospital room in which I was born.

The doctors waited a few days to allow the intravenous antibiotics to work in order to repair my right hand. Ultimately, that hand had narrow splints on each finger, and a half cast was placed from my palm to the top of my elbow. The splints were positioned such that a rubber band could be attached, so that eventually I would gently move or exercise each finger as therapy to regain mobility. My face laceration, about an inch above the top of the right side of my lip, was repaired by a plastic surgeon—beautifully, I always thought. Both legs had full-length casts after the breaks were fixed. My first questions were binary: Would I ever be able to play sports again, and what would be the longer-term consequences or limitations? Fortunately, after four months or so, I gradually was able to resume a normal life.

Those four months of recuperation were tortuous, not because of the recuperation process itself, but rather because my alcoholic mother demanded I be brought back to Fort Wayne to stay with her during convalescence. The choices seemed to me twofold and clear. I could have stayed with my father, who was a doctor and whose mother would delight in caring and cooking for me, or I could go to Fort Wayne to my mother's house, from which I had departed approximately eighteen months earlier.

I don't know why or on what basis the decision was made. Perhaps because my mother technically had custody of me at the age of seventeen, my father drove me to Fort Wayne. During the second day I was in Fort Wayne, my mother went on a drinking binge. I had not eaten or had anything to drink, couldn't walk, and couldn't use either hand. I didn't see her for thirty-six hours until she returned to me lying in bed, where I had urinated and defecated even though I had not eaten or drunk anything. Those were my last days in my mother's house.

High school, in short, was a very productive, expansive, and tumultuous time for me. On the athletic front, I was a member of the football team, on which I played quarterback and which was ranked number one in the state my sophomore year. I played on the basketball team, on which I was a guard and which played for the state championship at Hinkle Fieldhouse, site of the movie *Hoosiers*. I was selected to the all-city team in golf. On the academic front, I excelled and took mostly advanced placement classes. I thoroughly enjoyed school and felt fortunate.

Ken with friends in high school

The Collegiate

I applied to several colleges across the country, including Duke, Rice, and Washington University in St. Louis, but, for a variety of reasons, I eventually decided that I would attend Wabash College, an all-male liberal arts college of eight hundred young men in remote Crawfordsville, Indiana. I was offered some financial aid, although my father told me he would pay my tuition. Wabash was only an hour's drive to my father's house, and I was given the opportunity to work in my fraternity house kitchen, which afforded me some spending money. Additionally, Wabash was only a two-hour drive to see Lori, which I did nearly every weekend, and finally, my mentor at Wildcat Baseball was a current senior at Wabash.

I recall one weekend traveling to see Lori. To help pass the time on those road trips, I became moderately proficient at playing the harmonica. Anyway, it was the weekend before my first midterms at Wabash College. Upon arriving in Fort Wayne, I discovered Lori in the back of a van with an unknown dude in an uncompromising situation. It was obvious that they had been either drinking or smoking marijuana, and the two of them had been up to more than that.

I had nowhere to go and was in no position to drive back to college. Full of emotion, I drove to my mother's house to be with Duchess. I was greeted by my mother when I entered the house. That she was home was strange enough; that she obviously had been drinking was normal. She conveyed that my precious second Duchess had been killed by an automobile. My mother in her drunkenness had let Duchess outside in the front yard rather than in the fenced-in backyard. My initial reaction was to question when my mother was going to tell me. Didn't she have any remorse? Within thirty minutes,

I had been betrayed by my first true girlfriend and had now lost my best friend, Duchess. I was a total disaster. I lay in bed trying to cry myself to sleep. That didn't work, so I got out of bed and drove back to Wabash College in the middle of the night. Needless to say, my performance on midterms the next week was abysmal.

In the first semester of my second year in college, I received a telephone call from my mother's drinking buddy, Marge Keenan, who was in Fort Lauderdale, Florida. "Kenny, you need to get down here for your mother."

When I reached my mother, she was on the beach, gesturing about the ships on the horizon and the helicopter flying overhead. "Kenny, those are part of the Golden Protection Plan ordered by the president for you because of me." At dinner, I was seated under a can light, about which my mother remarked, "Kenny, you have to move your chair; those lights have deadly rays that are emitting on you." I schemed or tricked my mother by claiming I was sick, and, as a result, I was able to get her to take me to a hospital. While being evaluated privately, I conveyed to the doctor what was going on with my mother. She was subsequently placed in temporary custody at the hospital. Two days later, my brother, Matt, came to Florida and had her committed, since he was the required age of twenty-five, whereas I was eighteen at the time.

My modus operandi had developed into focusing on choices and what I could do rather than remaining stuck in the circumstances of what had happened and about which I had little or no control. I focused on school and was somewhat distracted with being on the golf team, with matches most weekends. During the middle of my sophomore year, because my grades rebounded greatly in the last one and a half semesters, I was presented the opportunity of a work-study program off campus the upcoming spring semester. I had three choices. I could study biology at Woods Hole in Massachusetts. Though seemingly dissimilar, I could study economics in Edinburgh, Scotland. Lastly, I could pursue prelaw working with juvenile gangs in Philadelphia. Later in life, upon reflection, I would have chosen Edinburgh, but in 1970, I chose Philadelphia based on the thought that if I pursued a career as a lawyer, I could help younger kids in trouble. I believed that my predicament growing up was not isolated.

In the spring of the next year, I went to Philadelphia with two other students, and we rented a small apartment that happened to be across the street from a playground which was the demarcation line for a gang's turf. On that playground was an indoor basketball court. I loved going into the gymnasium for pickup basketball games, and because of my background in basketball, I was well accepted even though I was the only white boy there. One day, when one of the opposing players went up for a shot, I blocked his attempt. That angered him. Maybe he felt diminished in front of his friends, although that was not my intent. In any event, he reached behind his trunks, pulled out a switchblade, and in one sweeping motion, opened the blade, which was directly pointed at me. A couple of the other players quickly restrained him by grabbing both arms and said to me, "Get out of here, dude, while you can." I ran immediately, never to return. Upon reflection, I thought because I was a good player, I had earned enough respect to generate the assistance in my escape. In any event, the basketball-turned-switchblade episode was a memorable first experience from my Philadelphia stint.

My eyes were opened during the Philadelphia days. During my first workday, I attended court. The defendant, Big Louie, was sixteen years old and probably around six feet, six inches tall. He had apparently stabbed a victim multiple times in the head with an ice pick during a gang scuffle. The victim was permanently paralyzed in a wheelchair and was in court. On another day in court, an assistant district attorney was prosecuting a custody case against an addicted mother who had grown impatient with the growth of her baby's hair. That mother had proceeded to literally sew a wig of sorts into the baby's scalp. That assistant district attorney was Lisa Richette, who had written *The Throwaway Children*, in which she discussed issues of juvenile justice and the law regarding juveniles. My experiences were numerous, and they gave me pause to consider that my life's background was mild in comparison to what so many of these kids were facing. In addition, it suggested to me that I might be able to help younger kids better and *before* they got into trouble if I were a teacher and coach rather than an attorney. More on that later.

I completed a long paper on my work-study program and returned to Indiana for summer school, during which I took twelve hours of classes and worked. After summer school, I returned to Wabash College. I petitioned the dean to allow me to try and take twenty-seven hours in the fall semester because, with such a course load, I would graduate in three years. My rationale seemed logical, and Wabash was expensive. In spite of my tumultuous first midterms after the loss of Duchess and Lori, I was performing at the dean's list level. In response to my pleadings, the dean agreed by imposing established checkpoints and clear-cut conditions.

Besides my degree, I left Wabash College with three significant takeaways. One, I had started college at age seventeen and subsequently graduated in three years and with a deepened sense of self-confidence emanating from the belief that if I applied myself with focus and tenacity, I could accomplish nearly anything. Two, I became the proud owner of the fraternity mascot, a mixed-breed dog, Gandalf, named after the wizard in J. R. R. Tolkien's *The Hobbit* and *The Lord of the Rings* trilogy. Gandalf was a most unique companion, and I always kept a picture of Gandalf and me gazing into each other's eyes hanging in my house. His stares into my eyes were a surreal form of communication. I could read his emotions, and he seemed to read mine. Gandalf was always present virtually anytime I left home. I took him on trips to the grocery, laundromat, walks at state parks, and simply everywhere. Before leaving Wabash, Gandalf and I challenged any two other fraternity brothers to a game of Frisbee. The object was to throw the Frisbee so it would land on the ground in the playing zone. Needless to say, Gandalf's agility and speed were unmatched. We never lost one game to any two other players, not even close.

Otherwise, I suppose the college days were largely typical. There were the usual pranks and experiences often coupled with alcohol at fraternity toga parties and some experimentation with marijuana and magic mushrooms. There certainly were many rock-and-roll concerts. My college years, 1969–1972, were during the heyday of hippies, peace, love, and rock concerts. Fortunately, my draft number for the

Vietnam War was two hundred eighty-seven, and that translated into meaning I likely would not be drafted.

The third takeaway from Wabash College was that my development was much more rounded, and I was well educated generally in liberal arts. I was familiar with American and world history, was conversant in American politics and philosophy, and grasped the fundamental concepts of English in terms of the structure of language as well as American literature and poetry. Of course, I had learned the fundamental concepts of algebra, geometry, and trigonometry, and I even had a rudimentary understanding of chemistry. I always took particular pride in the fact that I had graduated from college with honors in three years at the age of twenty. That accomplishment was something no one else could blunt, deflect, or minimize.

Gandalf and I headed to Indianapolis after graduation. I lived in a large, older house with five other men. My closest roommate, Doug, was a childhood friend who began work for an insurance company in Indianapolis and who had experienced the car wreck outside of Cincinnati with me. Another roommate was a young attorney who was beginning to build his practice on the southside of Indianapolis, and the fourth roommate ultimately became a federal judge. The fifth roommate was the heir apparent to a large pipe and valve company in Indianapolis, and the owner of a Great Dane. Though caged outside most of the time, he was the mascot of the Indy rugby team and, at times, a playmate with Gandalf.

My father lived in Indianapolis, and that was the reason for moving there. I began working in the Marion County government in the Department of Code Enforcement. I also enrolled in Butler University for my first master's degree and for certification to teach. I had the thought that if I became an attorney, I would only be able to help kids *after* they got into trouble. I wasn't confident of a career path in teaching and coaching, but I knew I enjoyed working with youth and felt I had something to offer. Perhaps as a teacher and coach, I rationalized that I would be able to help kids *before* they got into trouble. As mentioned, my Philadelphia experience birthed this thought.

During this time, I would go to my father's house for Sunday dinner. In this first year after Wabash, while doing master's work, I became close to Mamie, who taught me how to play poker and who demonstrated incredible agility with her cane as she periodically jabbed it in the air like a conductor as she spoke Italian to my father. Sometimes the tone of her speech indicated a mother's direction and perhaps disapproval. My father had been dating an Italian widow, Anna; and he would go to her house on Saturday nights for dinner. That seemed to bother Mamie. I suspected Mamie's angst was because my father, in her mind, should prioritize his mother. Late Sunday mornings typically included my cutting my father's grass with a push mower, the type with spinning blades, and then hanging out in the kitchen with Mamie, whom I watched intently numerous times making meatballs, pasta, antipasto, pizza, and the like. She would always give me, her little "Boo," careful instructions on her techniques, but more importantly, she would innocently and indirectly give me instructions in life along the lines of working hard, being honest, and treating people fairly.

Before dinner, my father would have his customary Jim Beam and Coke. I could always detect the acidity of Mamie's Italian rantings as measured by how many Jim Beam and Cokes my father had. Two drinks were acceptable or normal, but three drinks annoyed Mamie. All in all, my father was a dutiful son and took great care of his mother her entire life. Out of respect, my father waited for Mamie's passing in 1975, at the age of eighty-six, to marry Anna. With Anna, my father was able to enjoy the remaining years of his life, for which I remained grateful and pleased. My father and Anna moved to Sarasota, Florida, where he enjoyed his last six years of life. He passed in 1981, at the age of seventy-three. I was age thirty.

While completing my master's work, I was hired to teach government and coach as an assistant basketball coach and head golf coach at a suburban, well-established, and highly regarded high school. My life at that time ran down two parallel tracks: launching my career and falling in love. On one track, I began to date Dava, who was a senior at Butler University, where she majored in fine arts. The pursuit of a fine arts degree required Dava to attend some classes at the downtown campus of John Herron Art Institute. I was totally infatuated with Dava. She took me home to Rockville, a small town an hour or so west of Indianapolis, to meet her parents, who were kind people and ostensibly had a great relationship. The whole environment was like Mayberry in *The Andy Griffith Show*. They welcomed me, and this part of my life with Dava was absolutely progressing in positive terms. Dava was the first woman about whom I had fleeting thoughts about a long-term commitment and having children.

Unfortunately, those dreams were shattered. Mutual friends of ours from Butler University invited us over to dinner on a late Sunday afternoon. I was going to meet Dava there as she had some schoolwork to complete. I remember the appointed time came and went, and there was no Dava. This was in the days before cell phones. Needless to say, I had dinner with Dave and Carol, and Dava never appeared.

The next day, after teaching and coaching, I went to Dava's apartment. When I opened the door, I could hear voices in the bathroom: Dava was in the shower with one of her professors from the art school. Now I knew why she hadn't come to dinner at our friends'. I was devastated but immediately knew this was something I could not fix, nor would I even try. That episode pulled a major trigger for me: being betrayed and transforming that event into shame. I thought about the betrayal for some time, but I eventually was able to compartmentalize and move on. I developed a tendency that when I was finished analyzing a disturbing event, sometimes obsessively, I cast the event off to the side and built a silo thickly embedded in mental concrete. This behavior explained why my memories were sometimes difficult to recall and likely diminished or piecemeal. Being able to compartmentalize was a self-defense or survival mechanism I adopted, and prying open the concrete casing was sometimes too arduous and painful.

As far as my career path in general and coaching in particular, the basketball team was ranked number one in the state, and the team played in the final four at Hinkle Fieldhouse for the state championship. It was surreal to have played in the championship game when I was age fifteen and then later to have coached in the same venue. The golf team won the first trophy as conference champions for the high school, and we advanced to the state golf finals, where we finished in the top ten in the state as a team.

My juvenile antics also had a canvas during those years. For example, in basketball practices with the junior varsity, ages fifteen to sixteen, at 6:30 in the morning, I would have the players form a U around the free-throw area at the end of practice when the players were tired. They would shoot one free throw. If they missed, they took off an item of clothing. If they made the shot, they would simply rotate. Lo and behold, the tallest player on the team, Mark, missed a shot and only had his jock strap on when the gym door opened and the girls' team entered for their scheduled practice time.

Yes, I had a required visit with the athletic director later in the day and had to explain why in the world I did this. That meeting ended up with the athletic director not being able to conceal his laughter and saying it was the most creative technique he had ever heard to make young boys concentrate; but he also made me promise no more shenanigans. What the athletic director didn't know was that my arsenal was deeper than strip free throws. When the kids ran sprints around the retractable bleachers, they might just find their coach mooning them as they rounded the corner. Or, when coaching junior varsity in the county tournament, my line-up card given to the opposing coach included having one of my tallest, most athletic players, a six-foot, five-inch player, listed as a point guard. When the championship game started, the opposing team's point guard, maybe five-feet, seven-inches tall, was guarding my much-taller player, who was placed in the low post, which had been vacated by an offensive scheme pulling all other players outside by at least twelve feet. We simply fed the ball down to Eric, who had a ten-to-twelve-inch height advantage. That clairvoyance was worth an easy eight to ten points early in the game. The kids won the county championship, and we had a lot of fun. We shared mutual trust, respect, and the reciprocity of giving it our best.

Coaching golf had similar childlike behaviors. I generally rotated the players in my group so I could instruct them, and my group teed off first during practice rounds. An example of one of my favorite antics was to place a small garter snake in the golf cup after finishing putting so that when the following group putted, the first player to make his putt and reached into the cup to retrieve his ball was greeted by a snake. My group always waited on the next tee to see the sheer shock of the lucky player retrieving his ball. That player would be teased for days. The stories go on, but the gist was always to treat my players with respect, demand hard work, not accept deflection, and require that each reciprocated similarly with one another. In summary, the early years of my teaching and coaching were robust, enjoyable, and fulfilling. As with Joey in Wildcat Baseball, the kids gave me far more than I probably did them, but I gave teaching and coaching my all, and I cared deeply. It was not just a job to me.

At the beginning of my fourth year of teaching, a new high school was being opened, and I was asked to go there. I was that school's first graduating class sponsor, the assistant varsity basketball coach, the head golf coach, and a member of the first team-taught inter-disciplinary course. As the first such course in Indiana, the teachers combined the disciplines of art, English, and history/political science, which was my responsibility. The class met for two and a half hours per day, five days per week on a thematic basis.

Themes were varied and typically lasted six weeks. For example, in teaching the theme of conflict, we studied art like Picasso's *Guernica*, which depicted obvious conflicts in the style of painting, Cubism, as well as the dislocations and conflicts of war. Students read literature like Baldwin's *Notes of a Native Son*, which conveyed conflicts in the experience of an African American in early twentieth century America. We played exemplary music of the roaring twenties as well as presented an overview of the wave of immigration and World War I. It was simply unique to present a variety of academic disciplines within the context of themes. The class piqued a lot of interest, and we were invited to present at a national education conference at Notre Dame. The kids loved it, the teachers loved it, and we all learned immensely.

During the preceding summer, I was working in the golf program at a private golf club, Crooked Stick, that would host the PGA Championship in two years. So, a variety of high-level golf aficionados and wealthy members periodically played the course as a preview and planning exercise. Indirectly, this exposure planted a seed about the financial limitations of teaching and coaching. I purchased my first home, a three-bedroom bungalow on the north side of Indianapolis and centrally located between my father's house and the school where I taught. I remembered listening to Bob Dylan often at that time, so I renovated the upstairs of that house into a master bedroom complete with a brass bed as in Bob Dylan's "Lay Lady Lay." I also traded the Camaro for a silver convertible Jeep Wrangler, which was ideal for a fantastic vacation with Gandalf.

Gandalf and I left Indianapolis and headed westward with freeze-dried food, a tent, camping gear, and a couple of maps. There was no firm itinerary and only an estimate of six weeks in duration. Gandalf and I visited the Badlands, Yellowstone, Montana, and Idaho, then traveled down the West Coast from Washington through Oregon and past San Francisco to Southern California before returning through Utah and then a straight path back to Indiana. I recall many of those sites these many years later and never had any problems with Gandalf in spite of the bear, deer, coyotes, big horn sheep, moose, and other wildlife we were fortunate to see. Gandalf was so special.

Gandalf and I stayed with my mother's sister, Aunt Bobbie, for a couple of nights in Southern California. I hadn't seen Aunt Bobbie or my four cousins much for several years. In fact, I can only recall being around them a few times, but I had an unmistakable bond with my older cousin, Carol, and Aunt Bobbie. Many years after this, Aunt Bobbie called to convey she would be coming through Indiana and would love to see my two children and meet my new wife, Cindy. She was always gracious. What I didn't realize at the time of the meeting was that Aunt Bobbie was terminally ill, and this was her swan song of sorts. She was a truly special person with such class. I used to wonder what my life would have been had Aunt Bobbie been my mother.

Ken as young teacher and golf coach with the first-place trophy for the new high school

Ken and Gandalf

I Do

Prior to my fifth year of teaching and coaching, one of my students introduced me to a family friend, Jodi Thompson, and we began dating in the early spring of 1978. I was enamored by her looks and, at the time, enjoyed meeting and spending time with her mother, Donna. Jodi's parents had been divorced years earlier. Jodi was an only child, and her mother worked long and hard as a hairdresser, so Jodi was often left to fend for herself. Her father had long been absent, predominantly due to his alcoholism. There was so much I didn't know, but that would change later. By December, we were married. As I reflect back on the engagement and marriage, events happened far too quickly and without sufficient knowledge. I learned a life lesson, that **impulsivity can be friend or foe**.

In hindsight, I had fallen in love with the *idea* of marriage and children, not the person, all of which was not apparent to me at the time. For example, by early in the next year, after a few months of marriage, when we were living in my house, Jodi claimed she was allergic to Gandalf, and I needed to make *arrangements* for him. Donna, not Jodi, accompanied me to the Humane Society shelter, who promised me they would not euthanize him and would find Gandalf a good home—but that conversation was probably because I was crying uncontrollably. Donna tried to console me to no avail.

When at Donna's house, Jodi had interacted with and held her pug, Sugar, with no allergic reactions. Why was Gandalf a problem? That was a question I didn't ponder sufficiently, if at all, at the time. Taking Gandalf to the shelter was, without question or qualification, one of the three biggest mistakes of my lifetime, and that is something I have regretted for more than fifty years. In spring, as the class sponsor of the high school's first graduating class, I arranged the Gandalf Memorial Canoe Trip as a fond remembrance of and tribute to my four-legged companion and as a senior-year activity.

Knowing at some point that I would have a child or children, I wrestled with a career change. I wanted "more" for my someday children and hoped I could find a career that would provide not only financial potential but also freedom to spend time with my children, something I never experienced with my parents but which intuitively felt important. I became licensed and began to sell life and health insurance, an activity that was not all that uncommon in those days for a teacher/coach. Soon, I added securities licensing to the mix, and in the early years of my new career, I completed my second and third master's degrees in finance and insurance.

As bad as the Gandalf saga was, it was surpassed three years later, in the spring of 1981, when I won a free trip to a conference at the Copley Plaza in Boston, Massachusetts. I yearned to go to Boston to see the history I had studied at Wabash and for the content of the conference. This was my first noteworthy achievement of my budding financial services career. All expenses, including room and board, were provided. Jodi and I drove to Boston, and while registering, the desk clerk informed me that I had an urgent call from Anna in Florida. The desk clerk directed me to a private telephone and supplied the number I should call. Anna informed me that my father was dying and that he had asked for me. I thanked her and told her I was in Boston but would get there as soon as I could.

I turned to Jodi and said, "My father is dying. Anna says time is short. I am going to fly to Sarasota. You can stay here; everything is paid."

Jodi responded, "How can you abandon me?" A trigger of abandonment was pulled. I felt momentary shame, yet I needed to see my father in his last hours. I decided on a middle ground: I would drive for fourteen hours to take Jodi back to Indiana, then catch a plane from there to Florida. While driving west on Interstate 90 in Pennsylvania, I felt my father pass.

I stopped at the next roadside phone and called the number at which I had reached Anna a few hours earlier. "Kenny, I am so sorry.

Your father *just* passed." I was absolutely convinced my father wanted to tell me that he was sorry he was not more physically present in my life but that he was proud of me and that he loved me. While those words would have been heartfelt and meaningful, they were not necessary. **Actions speak louder than words.** Nevertheless, not seeing my father immediately before his death was the second-biggest mistake or regret of my life.

I had not grasped fully the meaning of straight commission when I started my career in insurance, although I was given some type of draw program that started at $1,200 per month and dwindled monthly to $0 in six months. To compound matters, Jodi and her mother, Donna, had decided that we needed a larger house. As a result, one was purchased on an inlet on a reservoir in South Harbor, which was twenty to thirty miles north of Indianapolis. The alleged rationale was that we would need a larger house since we would start a family, and Donna could live with us for a while to help with the finances and any baby that might come along. As with many things, it seemed to make sense in theory, but the size and price of the house, along with maintenance, was simply intimidating for someone starting out on a pure commission income format in selling life and health insurance. In all fairness, Donna did contribute; and for the year or so she was with us, it did work out.

A year or so after we moved to South Harbor, Donna married John Stader, known widely as the "Cowboy," while Jodi and I continued living in the house. Cowboy had grown up east of Indianapolis on a small farm and had been in trucking-related businesses, predominantly trailer sales for long-haul truckers. John's signature dress consisted of lizard-skin cowboy boots (of which he had many pairs), a black leather vest, a bolo, and, of course, a black cowboy hat. That hat hung in my office for many years after Cowboy's death, thanks to Damian.

The Cowboy's appearance may have been typical for western Texas or southern Arizona, but it was unique for midwestern Indiana. Beyond his appearance, Cowboy always presented a no-holds-barred and authentic self which was engaging, even captivating. He loved to attend motor vehicle racing events. One year, as he was walking through the garage area of the Indianapolis Motor Speedway during the annual 500 race, Cowboy—in his raspy voice—quipped to legendary driver A. J. Foyt, "By Gawd, A. J., I remember in 1971 when you made a gutsy move on the third turn on lap one hundred sixty-seven." From that moment forward, each year Cowboy was invited into A. J.'s garage, and the two of them would "build a scotch" and trade stories.

Cowboy told me repeatedly, "I'm not suggesting anything, but you need to be the most important person to *you* sometimes." His nickname for me was the Chiseling Dago because, in his mind, I handled his money more carefully and frugally than he did. In any event, Cowboy's witty but penetrating remarks were never-ending. For example, some of those quips included the following: "Dago, that suit looks like socks on a rooster" (I was wearing an Italian pinstriped suit with *larger*-legged pants), "Dago, you are too naïve, and I'm going to toughen you up," "It's a long ole road that doesn't turn," and "Dago, tell me what time it is and don't build me a clock."

John and I had many sessions together, and we would typically "build a scotch" for one another as the first step. Cowboy was indeed one of the most remarkable people in my life. He was much like my high school math teacher, Dick Sage, in that he was a gentle and kind man, and I knew he loved me and had my best interests at heart. He magnified another life lesson to me: **To thine own self be true, and it must follow, as the night the day. Thou canst not then be false to any man.** The Cowboy always presented his authentic self to me as well as to other people.

I remember years later when Donna passed. I was at my branch office in Evansville, Indiana, when I received a call from Cowboy to drive to his house as soon as possible. Donna was dying of cancer and was at home in bed. She apparently had been drifting in and out of consciousness. At one point, in an "out" moment, she muttered, "not yet, not yet," as if talking to the other side.

I arrived by her bedside, and Donna became instantly crystal clear and said, "Ken, is that you? Good. You'll never know what it means to me that you married Jodi." Donna passed within five minutes after those words. It would take years for me to more fully understand her comments, but Donna knew that I provided for my family, that I was always there, and that I was deeply involved 24/7 with both children. Donna also knew that Jodi never had a long-term, meaningful relationship with *any* other man, including her father, Floyd Thompson. Donna's passing was a blow that Jodi would never overcome. In fact, Donna's passing triggered a rapid and deep descent on Jodi's part. There was a similar spiraling down triggered in my daughter, Ashley, with Donna's passing because Ashley had been showered with affection and attention to an unhealthy level by Donna. Donna was Ashley's grand protector.

After Donna's passing, I recalled the last time I had spoken to my mother, during a lunch meeting I had requested. In advance of that meeting, I had written her a long letter in which I had opened my heart and soul in conveying that I had long forgiven her but that I could not forget so many things. I wanted a meeting to discuss a number of items. As was typical with her, at the lunch meeting, she deflected and simply said, "I did the best I could." There were never words to the effect of "I'm sorry you had so much emotional and/or psychological pain; I had no idea." There was no remorse whatsoever. This is one of the reasons why I strongly dislike deflection by other people.

Following the Florida Golden Protection Plan episode, and after no genuine discussion or remorse at our lunch meeting, I never spoke with or saw my mother again. I did not attend her funeral service years later, nor did my surviving brother, Matt. Tony had succumbed earlier. Understand that I believe, in her own way, my mother loved me; it is probably too painful to think otherwise. Nevertheless, in addition to her addictions, she had some mental illness: Some of her wiring was misconfigured. To continue the analogy, I knew that I was not an electrician and that I couldn't fix her addictions or mental illness. As she had mimicked to me a few years before from an Alcoholics Anonymous meeting, "You can't fix people, places, or things." This was one of many phrases she gleaned from Alcoholics Anonymous. She was adept at picking up phrases or words, but actions to support those words were always missing. **Actions speak louder than words.**

As an aside, I fully understand the power of addictions in general and to alcohol in particular. A lucky few are able to stop drinking, but often they become dry drunks because they haven't fully addressed and processed the root causes that generated their drinking. Those who quit drinking and recover in a more total sense are so few in number. That infrequent achievement of stopping drinking and addressing root causes is rare and among the reasons for my high regard for the therapist, Joan, whose involvement in my life would unfold in the years to come.

On many occasions, I believed in giving my mother not two or three but myriad opportunities for open dialogue to reach a mutual understanding. Similar aspects had been present in my relationships with Lori in high school and later with Dava, who was my second serious romance. I became black and white when it came to the necessity of relationships being built on trust, empathy, and compassion all couched in reciprocity. It was not a matter of being right or being the judge, jury, and executioner all at once. Rather, when maltreatment, deflection, and unrequitedness were consistently present in a relationship, I learned to sever those relationships as a matter of self-preservation, self-respect, and attenuation of emotional disruption.

Children

I have always thoroughly enjoyed reading the works of Khalil Gibran. From his poem "On Children":

> *Your children are not your children.*
> *They are the sons and daughters of Life's longing for itself.*
> *They come through you but not from you,*
> *And though they are with you yet they belong not to you.*
>
> *You may give them your love but not your thoughts,*
> *For they have their own thoughts.*
> *You may house their bodies but not their souls,*
> *For their souls dwell in the house of tomorrow,*
> *which you cannot visit, not even in your dreams.*
> *You may strive to be like them,*
> *but seek not to make them like you.*

Roughly twelve or so years before Donna's passing, Ashley Megan was born on September 20, 1980. During her early years, Ashley lacked any self-confidence because everything was done for her, particularly by Donna and generally by Jodi. In short, Ashley was too sheltered and too spoiled. Twenty-three months later, Christopher Damian was born on August 6, 1982.

Those next years flew by as monetary requirements increased beyond normal proportions, and my time became consumed entirely. This was why Cowboy conveyed I should take time for myself once in a while. I would drive for thirty to forty minutes to take the kids to a private elementary school, Park Tudor, in Indianapolis. I would then drive directly to work, where I would return client calls, telephone new prospects to set appointments, and have meetings with prospects and clients. In time, I would truncate my workday to pick up the kids, and, depending on the season, would coach Ashley's softball team or Damian's baseball team. I attended all their games *by myself*. In all of those years, Jodi attended only *one* of Damian's baseball games by sitting in her car parked beyond the center field fence. After the game, I would drive the kids home and often made dinner or, sometimes, picked up something on the way home. After dinner, I often did household chores like cleaning, laundry, or spending time with Ashley and Damian, be it helping with homework or simply interacting. I do not convey this type of schedule or narrative for any kudos. It simply was what my life had become.

Of course, the kids had a wide variety of pets. Each pet always started with the concept that having a pet would teach a young child responsibility, but I knew how that worked out. Over time, we had a golden retriever named Kabby, short for the German wine Kabinett, and a sheltie named Chablis. At the same time, we purchased a small collection of hermit crabs, one of which was absolutely huge, and Damian named it Brontosaurus. Eventually, we added three rabbits: Hershey, my brown, floppy-eared gem; Darth Vader, a black miniature rabbit for Damian; and Jordan, a white albino rabbit named after one of the band members in New Kids on the Block for Ashley. Of course, the rabbits had their own resplendent rabbit hutch.

Of particular note, as if the budding collection of animals was not enough, we additionally acquired two *male* chinchillas for Damian. Oddly enough, over time, those two male chinchillas produced several offspring until Damian figured out their genders and separated them. One of those chinchillas lived *well* beyond life expectancy and was a close companion to Damian for many years. For example, at Damian's beckoning, "Chilly" would sit on Damian's shoulder and eat pistachios one at a time from his hand. After Kabby and Chablis passed, two German shepherds were added to the menagerie. Heinz, a male, was for Damian. Heinz was a large, muscular German shepherd and was extremely intimidating by physical appearance alone to anyone who came to the door. Dresden, a female, had long, flowing, silky fur with pantaloons and was a beautiful shepherd with a sweet disposition. Dresden was for Ashley. Both were intelligent and athletic and seemed to watch over the menagerie with only mild disdain.

During those married days, we built three new houses with accompanying moves and decorating. We also traveled to the Caribbean and other places within the United States. I vividly recall the trip to Grand Turk where Cecil Ingham, owner of Sea Eye Diving, certified Ashley, Damian, and me in scuba diving, an activity we enjoyed many times and in many places over the years. I developed an interest in underwater photography, and some of those pictures of Ashley and Damian while scuba diving are among my favorites. The kids particularly enjoyed snapshots of me handling an octopus or a green eel as well as a variety of pictures of sharks, turtles, and barracuda. Jodi simply did not participate and wouldn't even go on the boat. This behavior was commonplace when it came to any activity of the kids, individually or together. Over those twenty years, I simply became deflated and worn out.

I reflect in particular on a couple of salient occurrences during those later days in my marriage to Jodi. One night, I spent hours on my hands and knees cleaning three thousand square feet of tile floor on the main level of our house. At the end of the cleaning, Jodi came by and said, "It looks like there is a streaked spot over there." Are you kidding me?

The next day, my mother arrived from Florida in typical fashion: She simply announced over a telephone call that she was coming to Indiana. That was a code phrase for she was going to stay with us. No questions were asked, and no permission was extended. While visiting, she would often go to an Alcoholics Anonymous meeting somewhere in Indianapolis. In any event, on that particular day, she had come home from an AA meeting with a couple of *friends* whom she had just met at the meeting. There was no notification, nor anyone's permission sought to bring people over.

It was raining, and apparently my mother proceeded to enter the house with her newfound friends, all of whom were wearing wet shoes. They proceeded to take a tour of the house with their shoes on. I was not home at the time. When I did get home at the end of the day, I immediately observed that all of the freshly cleaned tile had watermarks of footprints and dirt smudges. My clean floor lasted less than one day.

A second recollection is that the sales staff at a high-end retail store all knew Jodi because she was constantly buying high-end clothing and accessories. I remember one year asking her to sign our joint tax return and telling her she needed to curb her spending, especially since she did not work outside of the home after our first year of marriage. Jodi responded in a blurting fashion, "You need to make more money." My *adjusted* income that year was $514,000. When modified for three percent inflation, in the year 2023 that annual income would equate to $1,044,856. The attitude that she didn't need to curb her spending and that I needed to make more money astounded me for many years to follow.

During this same time period, I noticed a butcher knife under my daughter's mattress when I was changing sheets. I immediately called my and the kids' therapist, Bill Cook, who told me to take Ashley immediately to the children's psychiatric ward of a nearby hospital. As an aside, both Ashley and Damian had seen Mr. Cook and his partner, Dr. Beth, as had Jodi and I. In any event, we checked Ashley into the hospital, where she was restrained and evaluated over the next few days. Ultimately, the therapists suggested that we send Ashley to a boarding school, where she could process the turmoil largely stemming from the passing of her grandmother, Donna, and also sift through the dysfunction both at home and inside herself. Among the diagnoses was manic depression.

We chose Linden Hall, the oldest girls' boarding school in the United States, located in rural Pennsylvania. I also rented a horse, Sugar, for Ashley to develop riding skills in general and jumping in particular. Ashley excelled and apparently turned her attention outwardly to Sugar. Although extremely expensive, I always believed the boarding school experience saved Ashley from taking her own life. When Ashley returned home eighteen or so months later, she asked if we could buy her horse, Sugar, and bring her back to Indiana since Sugar was going into quasi-retirement at Linden Hall. I discussed that option with Jodi the next day when she returned home from another shopping episode. Jodi had spent an inordinate amount of money on shoes this particular venture and said "no" to Ashley's request. I told Jodi that Ashley's well-being was worth far more than a few pairs of shoes and would cost less than her shopping sprees. Needless to say, the hole in Jodi was deeper, more insidious, and more narcissistic than I had recognized.

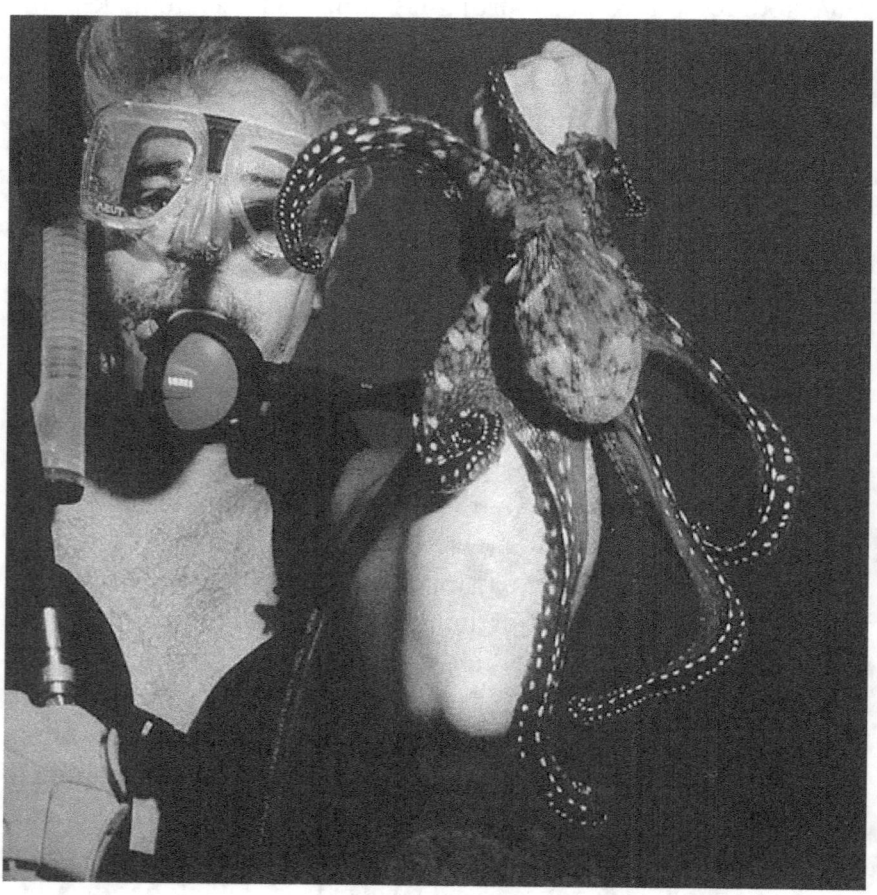

Ken scuba diving with octopus

Ashley scuba diving

Damian scuba diving

I Do Not

I recall one Friday evening a few years later when Jodi and I went out to dinner. I thought it important that we carve out one night per week among all the athletic and other school activities, let alone my work, to have an evening, or at least a couple of hours, to ourselves. Ashley and Damian were in their mid- to late teens.

At this point, I was head of a large financial services firm that had branch offices from southern Michigan to northern Kentucky. I was licensed in securities and insurance in all fifty states and had a fixed monthly business overhead of approximately $110,000. I also enjoyed the concurrent revenue.

In any event, after we ordered a glass of wine, Jodi, out of nowhere, said, "I think we should get a divorce." Without hesitation, I said, "We are. I'm filing Monday." This had never been discussed before, and I never knew what possessed Jodi to say what she did. I also don't know what made me say what I did, especially since, at that point in time, I always figured I could work harder and longer and simply do more to fix any problem.

The following Thursday night, Jodi cut her wrists. I called an ambulance, and Jodi went out by the pool with a semi-tourniquet I had fashioned. I was in the kitchen, where I could answer the door when the ambulance arrived and also keep an eye on Jodi, when Damian entered through the garage door, which opened into the kitchen. I told Damian that his mother had cut her wrists, that I had called an ambulance, that I couldn't be married to his mother any longer, and that I was going to file for divorce. I reassured Damian the divorce had nothing to do with Ashley or him, and I would remain as involved in their lives as I always had been. Most importantly, I conveyed that, no matter what transpired, I loved them both deeply. In reaction, Damian raised his arms straight in the air and proclaimed, "What took you so long?" He proceeded to give me a warm, firm embrace.

I needed to move out of the house. Ashley had an apartment I rented for her while beginning college classes. Damian was a senior in high school and could remain with his mother. I had no place to go and couldn't afford a second residence or even an additional apartment at that time. So, I was offered a place to stay at the home of my personal assistant, Susan, and her partner, Angie. During the initial part of laborious divorce proceedings, Damian lived with Jodi, and much to his chagrin, he became the proverbial man of the house. He went to the pharmacy for her antianxiety and other medications, to the grocery, and to wherever else his mother directed. Jodi became increasingly reclusive and dependent on Damian, and simultaneously, Damian's needs were not considered by her. I believe Damian was torn between feeling an obligation to his mother while knowing that living with her was not healthy for him.

Soon thereafter, one late morning, two executives from Massachusetts arrived unannounced in my office, and I was informed by those powers-to-be that I had a choice either to resign or to be terminated. I would find out later that one of them had a friend whom they wanted to sit in my chair as the boss. I was within *one* year of equity vesting of a multiple-seven-figure payout and had incredible expenses due to the divorce process. Those expenses included both sets of attorney fees, car payments, car and health insurance for Jodi, a monthly stipend for spousal maintenance, as well as all the utilities, taxes, insurance, and maintenance expenses of the so-called marital residence. So, I lost the company cash flow while simultaneously incurring incredible personal expenses. Worse than all of that, Damian stopped talking to me. That was far worse than all of the other events combined. Nevertheless, I sent Damian notes in the mail and tried to reach him by public phone so he couldn't identify me as the caller, often resulting in my leaving simple messages like "I love you, I miss you, and I will always be here for you."

Approximately six months later, my attorney told me I had to pay for Jodi's prescription for a sexually transmitted disease (STD) because the prescription was not covered by health insurance. That disbelief was erased by Damian calling me out of the blue the next day and saying, "Dad, I can't take it anymore."

I was fighting tears from hearing his voice, but I said, "You can't take what?"

Damian responded, "I can't live with Mom any longer, and I have nowhere to go." I told him I would rent an apartment the next morning, and we would live together, which was exactly what happened. I did not have copious amounts of money at that time; but I had a credit card, and my son needed help.

Soon after we moved, we received a voicemail message from Jodi that conveyed, "You guys are gay for living together." Obviously, her mental state had deteriorated significantly.

In time, the divorce was final, but my financial exposure was not. Jodi was required to have mental health evaluations twice each year by two independent psychiatrists. Of course, I was expected to pay whatever amount their bills indicated. I potentially was subject to *lifetime* spousal maintenance payments based on those evaluations. In short, I had exposure to deceit and manipulation.

After a month or two following the divorce edict in late July 2002, Jodi called my attorney directly and said something to the effect that if I were to pay her $5,000 in cash, she would never ask for another dime, and she would sign a document to that effect. I immediately told my attorney to draft the documents and to be sure that upon Jodi entering his office that two events had to happen. One, I would bring over a cashier's check with Jodi's name as the recipient, and the attorney should put it on the table in clear view of her. Two, I insisted that my attorney have two separate staff members talk with Jodi before he met with her in his office and that one of the staff members sat in his office during the actual meeting with Jodi. That way, those staff members could later testify, if need be, including whether their interactions with Jodi were normal and she appeared of sound mind.

The attorney told Jodi she could take the hold-harmless agreement to her attorney for review and counsel. Jodi saw the cashier's check, apparently viewed the check as compelling, and said a review by an outside counsel wasn't necessary. She took the check and signed the documents.

Apparently, Jodi had taken out a credit card and made purchases exceeding the card's limit, and creditors were pursuing her. Jodi also had done this in the last year of our marriage. I'll never forget the judge *awarding* (what a euphemism) me the six-figure indebtedness on credit cards that Jodi had taken out without my knowledge and run up. Unfortunately, when Jodi and I divorced, she burned my scrapbook filled with personal memorabilia from my childhood through high school days and refused to share any pictures, including the scuba diving pictures. All personal pictures of mine, including a few pictures of my father and mother, of my grandparents, of the children, and of the two Duchesses, were part of her blaze. Still, in those moments, I could only think, *I'm free at last, free at last.*

Damian and Ashley

Ashley, Damian, Sterling, and Walker

Damian, Ashley, and Ken

Moving on Up

I had the opportunity a few months after the hold-harmless episode to travel to Arizona and to be certified to teach Deepak Chopra's *Seven Spiritual Laws of Success*. I thought this was an opportune time, given my emotional state and turmoil in general, and I had read a large number of Chopra's books. In addition, I had long practiced transcendental meditation, which I viewed as the means of *listening* to God and the Universe, whereas prayer, to me, was *talking* to God.

There was a total of seven students: four from Europe, one from South America, and two from the United States. The first spiritual law of success was entitled Infinite Possibilities. Instruction and group discussion of the Law of Infinite Possibilities triggered my thinking on how I could benefit myself and others from the emotional, psychological, and financial challenges of divorce. After all, there were infinite possibilities. As a result, I became credentialed as a certified divorce financial analyst (CDFA) and began to network with family law attorneys.

My duties encompassed modeling divorce proposals in terms of the income tax and income-generation features currently and ten years into the future for each of the spouses. I included graphs which, in a picture, would identify how fair or balanced settlement proposals appeared to each side. Along the way, I did acquire new clients quickly and was able to empathize with the emotional and psychological challenges and dimensions of divorce as well as to help the clients focus on their overall financial health in the moment and in the future. I had no doubt about the immense benefit this consulting delivered to clients and advisors. It certainly provided immense benefit to me and was cathartic at the same time.

It took me about a year after the divorce was final to even entertain having a date with anyone. I spent my time building my personal practice and getting back into physical and emotional shape with the help of Mr. Cook. Eventually, though, I began to have dates with a large number and wide variety of women. At all times, I remained a gentleman, and the whole process was somewhat healing and certainly mind-boggling since I had not dated anyone in over twenty years.

I went through a lot of introspection, and my therapy sessions with Mr. Cook continued. Mr. Cook helped me fully understand that I hadn't done anything wrong—not only with Jodi but also my mother. In fact, he conveyed that I was the most romantic man he had ever known as well as being sensitive to the needs of others, and I was highly focused and accomplished. He made me aware that I was a highly sensitive person (HSP) and how to focus that sensitivity appropriately and within boundaries. We also explored the triggers in my relationships that stemmed in large part from my mother and identified characteristics in other people I should avoid.

I expressed my heartfelt appreciation to Mr. Cook by making him a framed, four-feet-tall by two-feet-wide triptych entitled *Touched by Angels*. I had taken underwater photographs over the years of three distinct varieties of angelfish, which had been preserved in slide form. I presented them to Mr. Cook in a beautiful frame along with a poem I had written. He honored me by prominently displaying *Touched by Angels* in his office for all to see.

The dating experience was at first a bit frightening because I harbored some serious trust issues from the events of Lori, Dava, and Jodi, let alone my mother. I was fifty-one years of age and had not been *out there*. Yet, I met some wonderful people and made a personal pledge that if there were not a genuine emotional connection after the initial couple of dates, I would not prolong dating that person.

Natalie was an attorney, and her father was a residential general contractor. I discovered after a relatively short period of dating that this relationship was not going anywhere. I simply was not feeling a growing attachment nor a deepening of emotion, and this was not a criticism of Natalie. It was simply how I felt. By analogy, oil and water are immiscible. They did not mix no matter how long I used a whisk. I was not ready for a more serious relationship with Natalie, or anyone for that matter. I had *the discussion* with Natalie. It didn't matter to her. The next morning, while living in the apartment with Damian, I was awakened by a pounding on the back slider. It was Natalie, who had come over to make a plea for us to continue dating. It was obvious: As a practicing attorney, she had planned and rehearsed her closing arguments. I was simply not interested; I was the proverbial hung jury. Later that morning, when I went to my car, I noticed a huge bow on the hood and a large teddy bear propped up and leaning on the windshield. It was Natalie's doing, and I was spooked because the apartment was within a gated community. I had visions of Clint Eastwood in *Play Misty for Me*.

Then there was the news anchor from one of the major television networks in Fort Worth, Texas. She had flown to Indianapolis for the weekend for our first meeting. I had an extra bedroom, and the plan was she would use it. I intuitively sensed while driving home from the airport, after having stopped at her sister's house for an hour or so, that this relationship was not going to work. My suspicions were confirmed when we got to my condominium, which I had purchased for Damian and me after the apartment living. Soon after arriving, she had opened her luggage to retrieve a half-gallon of vodka. Ultimately, I told her that I was sorry and that I felt our relationship was not going to work. Privately, I had experienced too many ill effects from alcoholism. I offered to pay for a room in a Hilton or to drive her to her sister's home. Neither offer seemed draconian to me, especially since her sister lived in Indianapolis, and they could spend the weekend together. However, I simply could not get rid of her; she lingered, pleaded, and then argued with an increasingly uncomfortable amount of vehemence while all of the time drinking the vodka. *Hours* later, I took her to a Hilton and once again was free at last.

One other relationship bears recounting: Jeanine. Jeanine was divorced and lived with her grown daughter, who was working on her master's degree in psychology. Jeanine was more than comfortable financially. After dating a couple of months, she asked me if I wanted to meet her in Sydney, Australia, where she would be with two girlfriends and one of the girlfriend's husbands at the end of a month-long trip. The four of them were traveling to Japan, Vietnam, Cambodia, and then ultimately to Sydney. All of us would share a large condominium and have about five days in Sydney during the World Cup soccer championship between Australia and Britain. I said yes. The airline ticket was significant for me because when my divorce from Jodi was final a few years earlier, my net worth was a *negative* $650,000, and I had been working diligently to erase that debt. Nevertheless, I agreed to the rendezvous in Sydney.

The first night was anxious because Jeanine and I had not been intimate. When Jeanine exited the bathroom and came to bed, it was obvious to me that virtually her entire body had been touched by a plastic surgeon, and the amount of plastic surgery turned me off. I was concerned that if her body were so manipulated, then perhaps she had other issues, and I wanted nothing to do with those potential issues.

We then had to spend the next five days together, and I tried to make the best of it. We walked over the *top* of the Sydney Harbour Bridge strapped in harnesses, visited Bondi Beach, and, of course, went to the other tourist sights of Sydney. Dinners were a group event, so that took some pressure off. The lack of intimacy was apparent. I cannot tell you accurately the depths of drudgery while flying home from Sydney to Indianapolis over twenty hours nonstop and not saying more than ten words in total between us.

When Jeanine's daughter picked us up at the airport and asked how the trip was, Jeanine said accurately and curtly, "It was horrible." Nothing else was said by anyone, and the tension in the air was obvious. The drive from the airport to Jeanine's home was excruciating and one of the longest thirty minutes of my life. Upon departing the car at Jeanine's home, she said, "You can pick up your luggage here tomorrow. I will put it out on the front porch." Those were the last words spoken between us. I had repeated a cardinal sin: I had become enamored with the *idea* of a relationship with Jeanine and the consequent trip to Sydney without really knowing her. A trigger had been pulled, and the gun shot me again. **Impulsivity can be friend or foe.**

I began to think about my impulsiveness and the problems it created in the dating world. I thought it would be better if I met potential dates by first having some kind of common experience like scuba diving, teaching, golf, and so on. I also knew that I did not want more children, nor did I want to raise someone else's children. In my mind, I was simply too old to raise, let alone produce, additional children, and I didn't have the emotional energy. It didn't seem fair that I would potentially be at a child's high school graduation when I was seventy years of age.

Then I had the idea that I should ask the woman who was cutting my hair if she knew a woman whom I might enjoy meeting. After all, I rationalized that the relationship between a hairdresser and a woman was often a powerful connection. The woman who cut my hair, Kim, knew me somewhat and, given that knowledge, might be able to assess a potential fit. So, I asked her, "Do you know anybody I might enjoy meeting?" Immediately, I added, "Let me bring a poem in next time and read it. Then you'll know much better exactly what I'm looking for: someone who is touched by this particular poem." Here are a few excerpts from "The Invitation" by Oriah Mountain Dreamer:

> *It doesn't interest me what you do for a living.*

> *I want to know what you ache for, and if you dare to dream of meeting your heart's longing.*

> *. . .*

> *It doesn't interest me what planets are squaring your moon. I want to know if you have touched the center of your own sorrow, if you have been opened by life's betrayals or have become shriveled and closed from fear of further pain. I want to know if you can sit with pain, mine and your own, without moving to hide it or fade it or fix it.*

> *. . .*

> *I want to know if you can see beauty, even when it's not pretty, every day, and if you can source your own life from its presence.*

I want to know if you can live with failure, yours and mine, and still stand on the edge of the lake and shout to the silver of the full moon, "Yes!"

It doesn't interest me to know where you live or how much money you have. I want to know if you can get up, after the night of grief and despair, weary and bruised to the bone, and do what needs to be done to feed the children.

As I was reading the poem out loud in its entirety, Kim's hairdresser partner, Sonya, walked to our chairside, looked at Kim, and said, "Cindy!"

Kim said, "Absolutely." So, the next day, Kim called her client, Cindy, and said that she wanted Cindy to meet me. Cindy said she would have to think about that, as she had just emerged from a horrible, even abusive, relationship and that she didn't think she ever wanted to meet another man. In fact, she was trying to figure out how to move with her younger, eighteen-year-old son, Sean, to Arizona, where she had attended school and was generally familiar. A few days later, Cindy agreed to meet me and thought, at the very least, she would get a free dinner.

We met on January 20, 2004, at a small locally owned restaurant called Café Nora, which was not far from where Cindy was living. We had a robust and long conversation. Given our backgrounds, we delicately but directly questioned one another over the bigger issues, such as whether or not we wanted additional children, our morals concerning honesty and fidelity, our personal goals and dreams, and the like. We were both old enough and experienced enough to not waste time. Cindy was content to be by herself at that point for the rest of her life. She didn't need to have a partner. In fact, she thought that having a partner would likely not happen, and that was fine with her. I was not nearly as resolute. The conversation flowed smoothly and warmly the entire night, and we were eventually informed that the restaurant was closing.

I was totally enamored with Cindy. She was beautiful and carried herself well. She was direct but polite, well educated, and had lived in a variety of places in and outside of the country. In fact, her father had been in the foreign service, and her family had lived in Lima, Peru, from Cindy's ages eight through twelve or thirteen. This is where Cindy's ear for language was developed and perhaps a reason why she would eventually teach, among other things, Spanish. Both of her parents, but particularly her mother, were fascinated with language. In fact, her mother spoke and read several languages; and in part due to her father's foreign service career, Cindy's family traveled extensively, hence forging Cindy's love of language, travel, and her adventuresome nature.

Prior to our first meeting, Cindy had lived on St. Croix with her two sons, Jesse and Sean. What took Cindy to St. Croix from Texas was the opportunity to be a partner in a pub plus a potential romantic interest. Upon moving her sons and loyal companion, Bailey, a yellow lab of immense kindness and heart, she soon discovered the romance was going nowhere and the pub partner had problems with a drug addiction.

She had long ago divorced the father of her two boys for a variety of reasons, and now found herself on an island, by herself, and needing to feed and house her two sons and Bailey. That responsibility eventually led Cindy to having three jobs and working seven days a week, and that spoke volumes about her character, resolve, and intestinal fortitude. It also made perfect sense why the phrase in "The Invitation," "I want to know if you can get up, after the night of grief and despair, weary and bruised to the bone, and do what needs to be done to feed the children," resonated so deeply within her and likely had piqued her interest enough to simply meet me. I am confident she wanted to verify if I were simply spewing a message like some kind of bait or if I really believed those sentiments.

I was totally engrossed with Cindy after our first meeting, but I recalled how at least twice before, with Jodi and Jeanine, I had acted too quickly, too impulsively, and later paid the price. One week after our first date, on January 27, Cindy called Kim to ask if she had heard from me concerning our first date. Kim responded "no," and Cindy was perplexed, since she believed we had a wonderful first date and shared values and perspectives important to each of us. Serendipitously, within five minutes of Cindy hanging up with Kim, I called Cindy. I had no idea she had talked with Kim, and I had called simply to convey that I had a wonderful time meeting her and to ask if she wanted to have another date.

One of our first dates was my cooking for Cindy. I had purchased a copy of the book *The Invitation*, wrapped it, and placed it under her plate as a surprise gift. I had prepared a tossed salad with boiled shrimp arranged so that the ends touched and formed the image of a heart. The main course was fresh fish topped with a kind of homemade salsa and baked inside parchment paper. I knew Cindy liked seafood, and I suspected the salsa would be appealing too, since she had lived many years in Texas. I took time to pair wine with our meal. Of course, our conversation started quickly and flowed throughout the evening. I know Cindy enjoyed herself and thought maybe I was different in a good way from previous relationships. In fact, Cindy later would convey to me that she had wondered if I were gay. I continued to laugh for years in recalling her initial thoughts, but that was what she questioned. I knew that she was unique and felt there was potential for a meaningful, trustworthy, and long-term relationship.

In any event, there were no more delays in asking Cindy out again and again. At this point, her younger son, Sean, was moving to Las Vegas to be with his older brother, Jesse. Cindy was teaching and caring for her two dogs, Bailey and Java. Cindy had rescued Java as a newborn pup with her siblings from a dumpster on St. Croix. She found homes for the other puppies and kept Java for Sean. With Sean's impending departure to Las Vegas, Cindy had flexibility with her time and guardedly looked forward to exploring, perhaps for the last time, a potential and meaningful relationship. I was living in the condominium that I purchased after the initial postdivorce apartment, and Damian, of course, was living with me. Cindy and I attended the symphony, modern dance performances, sporting events, and even went on a picnic to Eagle Creek Park, for which I made tuna salad, a favorite of Cindy's, and brought smoked gouda cheese, crackers, grapes, and wine.

At other times, Cindy and I took walks with Bailey and Java and sometimes just hung out, drank a glass of wine, and talked. These were truly magical days for me and refreshing to Cindy that a guy would be attentive, pay for things, and seemingly was honest. I knew Cindy did not have much financially because she supported her two boys their entire lives without any contribution from their father. For that matter, he never even changed a diaper. In fairness, he simply had not wanted children. Regardless, a couple guys Cindy had dated, particularly the most recent one before me, weaseled what money she had by saying things like "Hey, you get this, and I'll pay you back." The paybacks apparently never happened. I was not flush with cash either, as I was working my way back from the divorce and was focused toward reducing my staggering amount of debt, but I always paid for all things for Cindy and me. It was the right thing to do in my mind. Nevertheless, we had each other and truly enjoyed each other's company. Spending time together was more than enough and generally more relaxing, engaging, and fulfilling than time spent with anyone else either of us had experienced.

Ten or so months later, I asked Cindy if she, including Bailey and Java, wanted to move in with me, and she said yes. While Cindy had a significant distance each morning to travel from the condominium to the school where she taught in Zionsville, my schedule allowed me to walk Bailey and Java, so my bonding with the dogs grew as it did with Cindy. For that matter, both my children got along well with Cindy. Things were going great, and Christmas was fast approaching. In fact, Cindy and I added a business partnership to our evolving personal relationship. We were partners in a tutoring program for kids of all ages and subject matters. It was an opportunity for both of us to supplement our incomes and to work together on a common purpose. We spent parts of weekends interviewing prospective tutors, and since I had taught, my input was of some value. Cindy was responsible for interviewing prospective students and their parents, hiring and then scheduling tutors with students, garnering feedback, and logistical aspects. My role was predominantly to handle billing to students or parents, keeping track of payments, maintaining the financial records, and the like.

Christmas season was enjoyable and refreshing compared to earlier ones I had experienced, particularly from my previous married years. Yet, my biggest trigger was pulled when my mother called *late* on Christmas Day. The content of conversations with my mother was always the same, and the tone was always glum. There were always the same topics and the same words, and it was always all about my mother. "Kenny, I have been doing this or that; my back has been sore; what's going on in the markets, etc." There was never a question about me or what might be happening in my life. *Are you settling after the divorce? Are you dating anyone? How are the kids? How is work?* Nothing about me. The sheer *sound* of my mother's voice sent me spiraling.

My emotional reaction to my mother's call was to immediately erect psychological walls and to withdraw inside of myself. It was like an alarm for self-defense went off. That's when I made the *biggest* mistake of my life. I asked Cindy to move out! It has always been exceedingly difficult for me to reflect, recall, and write about this transgression. My request of Cindy moving out was a *horrible* mistake generated out of a purely triggered emotional response to all the trauma and turmoil my mother presented me over the years. Those past events and associated feelings were deeply embedded in my being. Misguidedly, I projected those emotions and let them flow over onto Cindy.

It certainly didn't take long for me to realize that I had overreacted emotionally, thrown common sense to the wind, and made a horrific request. Cindy had nothing to do with my mother, and my mother had nothing to do with Cindy. In fact, my mother knew nothing about Cindy and didn't even know we were dating, let alone living together.

I called Cindy about a month later after continuously trying to process what was going on with me and pondering why in the world I would let an emotional reaction to my mother trigger such a horrible consequence. I asked Cindy if she would be willing to meet me for a cup of coffee the next morning, a Sunday. She had a one-word response, "Why?" I said that I *really* needed to talk to her and begged for that one cup of coffee together. Thank God, she agreed.

So, we met the next day, and I apologized for my horrific, emotional action, conveyed that I missed and loved her, and asked her if we could date again. Cindy was hesitant for obvious reasons, but eventually she relented under one nonnegotiable condition: I had to see and work with her therapist, Joan, for a long period of time and that I agreed Joan and Cindy could talk about relevant parts of those therapy conversations. Not only was that fair in my mind, but it struck me as being very wise. Internally, I was jumping for joy, and I called Joan first thing Monday morning.

Joan and I met for our first session on February 8, 2006. Joan was a recovering alcoholic of many years, which I construed as a significant attribute for me, given my mother's background, but Joan's intuition and professionalism extended well beyond those boundaries. Even in that first session, Joan identified that I was people-pleasing and had low self-esteem stemming from abandonment issues which manifested in feelings of shame. These were sources of self-sabotage and began to explain my reaction to my mother's call on Christmas evening and asking Cindy to move out.

I saw Joan weekly thereafter, and we made rapid discoveries—and hence progress—over a lot of tears. We identified that when something did not work for me, I tended to internally move from "I made a mistake" to "I *am* a mistake" due to triggering past "hooks" or wells of unresolved issues. Joan helped me understand that the origins of my shame, in part, were based on the fact that I had needs, and mine had largely been unattended and even ignored. Joan explained that critical parents, like my mother, would deny my needs, and the belief that something must be wrong with me became internalized. Joan conveyed that one key when using self-talk was for me to identify signs and symptoms (wells, hooks, triggers) and then to separate fact from fiction, which was often emotion-based.

Joan further explained that when my shame was triggered, to get out or escape, I would act with compulsive behavior to anesthetize my feelings. Furthermore, working on shame triggered more shame, so my recovery was about (a) careful, deliberate, and mindful breathing; (b) reconnecting with myself, God, and others; (c) focusing on facts, not fictions; and (d) expressing emotions. My emotions were highly elevated. In fact, Joan conveyed that I was a highly sensitive person (HSP), a marker Bill Cook had identified earlier. Joan said that my shame suggested I didn't have needs. In my shame, incidents occurred, and no one intervened to say, "Yes, it was terrible."

My clear directive from Joan was to eliminate toxic relationships, as they would obliterate my emotional homeostasis and deeply cloud my rationality, which would lead to making decisions or taking actions I would later regret even more. Under those conditions, other most-valued relationships could be wrongly sabotaged. For me, particularly through the help of Mr. Cook and Joan, my prescription was as follows:

(1.) Identify triggers;

(2.) Use self-talk tools;

(3.) Separate facts from emotions;

(4.) Demand reciprocity;

(5.) Don't let people walk over me;

(6.) Recognize I can't fix other people;

(7.) Establish boundaries based on facts without qualification; and

(8.) Avoid at all costs other people who

    (a.) lack empathy;

    (b.) are all talk, but no action (even if they say nice things);

    (c.) operate on the format that I give and they take;

    (d.) repeatedly pull my triggers; and

    (e.) have issues with alcohol and/or drugs.

I found it interesting that my prescriptive course was largely based on *actions* rather than words, like a mantra of sorts. No one suggested that those prescriptive behaviors applied as screens or filters for people in general. Rather, based on *my* personal characteristics of sensitivity, general compassion, and generosity, coupled with the betrayal I felt and experienced with my mother, Jodi, and to a lesser extent, Lori and Dava, they were simply personality traits in some people I should avoid.

All five of these behaviors were evident in spades with my mother. Joan and Mr. Cook both conveyed in no uncertain terms that it was legitimate and healthy for me to cut off the relationship with my mother after so many attempts to have meaningful discussions, and doing this would give me a clean slate with Cindy as well as others. I thought I could overcome these behavioral traits and could *fix* them with extreme kindness, generosity, and effort. I was wrong in those beliefs. Those prescriptive boundaries were immensely helpful and aided me in avoiding sabotaging and debilitating relationships in the future. Consequently, I was able to heal emotionally more quickly and to expend energy more positively and productively with others, my work, my children, and, of course, Cindy.

Needless to say, Joan and I increased our sessions to twice per week because I trusted her, I was evolving positively, and I truly believed Cindy was special. I clearly remember Joan telling me that Cindy and I were *compatible*, a key component of any meaningful relationship offered by the Cowboy earlier in my life. Additionally, Joan observed that while I was more verbose, Cindy would speak her mind and that we both had triggers. How I acted could overcome my triggers, and thereby I would be able to offer a more consistent and authentic self to Cindy. I was forever grateful to Mr. Cook and Joan. They, in fact, saved my life as well as my relationship with the love of my life, Cindy.

I Do, Act Two

Cindy and I continued dating; my triggers became less sensitive, and our relationship deepened. We took a trip to Puerto Vallarta, and one night we walked a fair distance up the terraced street to a rooftop restaurant. The mountains were behind us, and the bay was in front of us. All of the surroundings were illuminated by a bright moon in a clear sky. We enjoyed all the homemade tequila we wanted and a very large platter of delectable fresh seafood, including a centerpiece of grilled huachinango surrounded by langostinos, large prawns, oysters, and the like.

Upon returning to our hotel room, as we looked out past our balcony full of bougainvillea onto the moon-draped ocean, Cindy said, "It doesn't get any better than this, does it?"

I said, "Yes it does," as I dropped down on one knee, reached in the pocket of my cargo shorts, and presented Cindy with a heart-shaped diamond in a traditional engagement ring setting and the words "Will you marry me?"

We planned our wedding to be at the Stratosphere in Las Vegas on October 14, 2006. Cindy's two sons lived in Las Vegas, and it was a destination that our small, intimate group of friends, my brother, and my children particularly enjoyed attending. The night before the wedding, we were able to host a dinner for our small group of twelve or so at Paris Las Vegas. Our intent was to thank all for coming and to share our mutual love. Cindy and I were shocked and so touched at the conclusion of that dinner when my dear friends, Jerry and Ricky, secretively picked up the entire tab, including drinks, as a wedding gift.

Not long after our marriage, we sold the condominium and bought a house on Brave Court in Lawrence Township, where I had previously taught. We both thought it a good idea to remove the condominium from our consciousness, given it was the situs of my biggest mistake. A larger home would be more comfortable for all of us—including Bailey and Java, as they would have a fenced-in backyard. The benefits of the house included immediate access to a nature trail, which was ideal for Bailey and Java, and a walkout basement large enough to feature a sitting area for a large television, my desk and files, a bar, a dartboard, a pool table, storage, and a fourth bedroom and bathroom.

Ashley and Damian would come over somewhat routinely. Cindy and Ashley would play darts; Damian and I would shoot pool. Given the layout of the area, we were all able to talk among ourselves and see what each other was doing. At times, Ashley would bring her twin boys, Sterling and Keller.

The twins and I would play "dinosaur," a goofy game where I would run and hide somewhere in the house and the twins would come looking for me. When they were approaching me in hiding, I would jump out and make a loud dinosaur noise (whatever that was) and wave my arms. The twins would squeal with a combination of fright and delight. Those days were fun-filled and beneficial to all of us becoming closer.

Ashley's first marriage would soon end. Given the loss of her grandmother (Jodi's mother, Donna), Ashley had begun a deep, psychological downward spiral. Quite frankly, she became out of control, as evidenced by promiscuous dating, abundant drinking, increasing cursing, excessive tattooing, and generally becoming more and more irresponsible.

Ashley would not take her medications and denied she had any problems. I was reminded of the previous prescription I had been given about people with certain behavioral traits (lack empathy, all talk, give/take, etc.) that clearly now applied to my own daughter. I was reminded to separate facts from emotions, to seek reciprocity, to not allow Ashley to walk all over me, to recognize I couldn't fix Ashley's problems, and to establish boundaries based on facts without qualification.

Ashley refused to see any type of mental health professional. Her spiraling out of control continued. It saddened Damian and me that we had no relationship with Ashley for many years. She had been married three times, divorced three times, and had five children with three different baby daddies. She had gained considerable weight, and tattoos covered most of her body, arms, and legs. All of this was sad but true.

She had also cut out of her life and the lives of her children people who genuinely cared for them. Beyond Cindy, Damian, and me, the exorcised group included the twins' father and all sets of grandparents from her three marriages. Severance from one of those grandparents, Deb McWhorter, who was Ashley's second husband's mother, was particularly abhorrent. Deb had always welcomed the twins to her home and on McWhorter family events like cruises, visits to Mississippi family reunions, and so on. More importantly, Deb was one of the sweetest, kindest, and most nurturing people in the lives of the twins. The consequences on the children were dreadful. I remain thankful that I maintained a good relationship with Deb and the second husband, Matt, who was a really good guy and an outstanding father to my grandson, Walker. Walker was a wonderful child. He was accomplished at baseball as a catcher and batter and, more importantly, developed into a nice, well-adjusted young man, largely due to his exceptional father and Deb.

Something had to be done. Cindy, Damian, and I met Ashley at a McDonald's for an informal intervention of sorts. Within five minutes of our meeting, even though there were many people in the restaurant, Ashley stood up and let it rip with utterances like "You cunt-ass; fuck you" to Cindy; "You're a loser" to Damian; and "You never did much of anything for me" to me. Her outburst concluded with "Fuck all of you. I don't need you." She walked out of the restaurant, and despite future attempts by Damian and me to repair our relationships, they were forever broken.

Ashley's assertion that I never did much of anything for her cut deeply. I had committed one hundred percent of our resources toward her therapy, including, though not limited to, Linden Hall boarding school. In addition, when she was much smaller, I was her playmate at times in playing My Pretty Pony, and I was frequently the guest of honor at her tea parties for two. Ashley had a toy stove and would prepare tea for us. Mimicking a waitress and wearing a pair of her mother's old high heels and a child's apron, Ashley would deliver the tea, saying with an adorable smile, "Daddy, here is your tea!" I played along and responded, "Ashley, this is the best tea I've ever had! May I have some cream?" That would delight her as the fantasy would continue.

As Ashley became older, I was heavily involved in her softball and basketball endeavors. She often had friends over to our house to swim, and I always cooked hamburgers and hot dogs on the grill for all of them. She would bet her friends, male and female, that none of them could beat us in billiards. Consequently, I played many pool games with Ashley as my partner, and we never lost a game, which fueled more invitations. Eventually, in her young adulthood, I even tolerated, for a period of time, meeting a variety of men she dated. Those meetings stopped when one of them used the snowplow on his truck to barricade my garage door at the Brave Court house with five feet of snow so I couldn't leave my house. As a last example, I funded college education accounts for each of the twins, which Ashley later cashed out for a trip to Europe with one of her future husbands. To have heard "You never did much of anything for me" was not only unrealistic but deeply hurtful.

Conversely, Damian had lived with me for a number of years in the condominium through the final two years of the divorce process. As Cindy and I planned our Las Vegas wedding, Damian rented a meager half of a double and enrolled in the local university for a degree in biotechnology. In his earlier years, Damian had been very active in athletics, and I had the pleasure of coaching his baseball and basketball teams. He was accomplished in basketball, football, and baseball, but one night at dinner, Damian remarked, "I don't know if I want to keep playing sports."

Immediately, Jodi said, "You don't have to." I thought this was a bad decision, as his physical development, social interactions, and experience of life's lessons were very positive through the teams on which he played. Yet, as was often the case, when the parents were divided, the child would exploit them not being on the same page, so

Damian ended his formal athletic endeavors. I was concerned how Damian would spend his newly found available time.

When Damian was approximately five years old, we often would play dinosaurs. Of course, he had complete sets of the figures and children's books about them. One of Damian's favorite early childhood memories revolved around my buying a Slip 'n Slide, a three-feet-wide by twenty-feet-long plastic strip that was designed to be placed on a gently sloping hill. A water hose was connected at the top which allowed the plastic to remain slick. I pointed in the woods and said to Damian, "Look over there, carefully, at that animal." He took the bait and was surveying the woods when he heard me laughing uncontrollably as I slid naked down the Slip 'n Slide.

I am not suggesting that Damian never got in trouble. He did, but most of those occurrences were innocuous and typical for his age. To note, while in high school, Damian was picked up for tagging with spray paint some property in the Broad Ripple area on the north side of Indianapolis. I drove to get him while he was being detained informally by the local police. I simply asked Damian, "Did you learn your lesson?"

He said, "Yes," and that was the end of that event. Damian would not lie to me, and he knew I would always be transparent with him.

There were other examples, but, all in all, they were minor; and Damian seemed to learn from each episode. Damian never asked for much at all. Rather, he was always willing to help. I recall when his mother, Jodi, in a clear display of mental imbalance, instructed that Damian and I supply feeding stations for the birds and wild raccoons in our area around the house. Those so-called feeding stations were provisioned with Hostess Twinkies, Rice Krispies Treats, miniature marshmallows, and Corn Pops: an amalgamation of the unhealthiest foods that somehow seemed appropriate to Jodi and would certainly be welcomed by the raccoons. This was a window into Jodi's mental health. Worse than replenishing the raccoon stations with this kind of menu was periodically cleaning the areas around the feeding stations. That kind of diet was not conducive to good health for a raccoon, or anything else for that matter, a fact about which Damian and I were reminded every cleaning session. Damian always helped, and we sometimes reflected on how we shared our mutual lament about the raccoon duties.

One early evening while replenishing the raccoon supplies, we noticed an ill possum lying on its side and largely listless. When Damian informed his mother of the spiritless opossum, she insisted we take the opossum for treatment to our friend, a veterinarian. Roger remarked he had no experience with opossums (how could he?) and asked what we wanted him to do. I asked him to euthanize the poor thing to put it out of its misery, and I would gladly pay for all services. Roger, Damian, and I agreed we would not tell Jodi. Rather, we would simply convey that Roger took care of the opossum.

While Damian was living in very meager conditions while pursuing his college degree, I paid for the basics, like rent, utilities, and some spending money for groceries; but Damian never asked for more. He always said, "I'm fine." Rather, he would choose to eat ramen noodles and get by; it was a matter of pride and empathy. His focus was on obtaining his undergraduate degree. He believed the quality of his life would improve in time, and his current conditions were temporary and manageable.

One late spring semester, he asked me if I knew of any job openings for the summer. I asked my dear friend, Jerry, if he was hiring in his commercial construction business. Jerry said, "Yes, but Damian will be on a shovel for most of the summer, and it's tough work, especially in the heat." Damian jumped at the opportunity because the hourly pay was much more than his alternatives, like working at a gas station or convenience store. Damian remained in that company for many years as a vital member of management. His learning was incredible as he became facile in how to operate the CAD system, programed software for the large equipment, drove/operated all of the heavy and not-so-heavy machinery, quoted large jobs, and more. Damian loved his work and the people around him, as they did Damian.

Damian had diligently established solid 401(k), Health Savings Account, and personal portfolio and savings programs. He understood the time value of money. Furthermore, he became interested in diet and physical development. For many years, he lifted weights six days per week and developed an incredible general state of mental and physical health and fitness. Of equal pride to me, Damian maintained deep friendships, both male and female, from many years in his past and demonstrated sincere altruism and empathy in those relationships. He was always altruistic by nature and sought to help others.

Damian also couldn't stand to see a cat on a jobsite abandoned, so when he saw one, he adopted it. Not wanting that cat to be alone, he procured a second cat. Bud and Meatball provided good companionship to one another for many years as well as joy to Damian. Furthermore, Damian had been able to process his mother's and sister's "conditions" and refused to re-engage until either had admitted her role or medical condition and sought help. However, in observing his mother and sister, and because of a previous personal, dishonest romantic relationship, Damian's focus on finding a lifetime partner and perhaps having his own children took a back seat to his career and personal development. He remained open to the possibilities of a life partner, but he was not actively looking as some kind of self-imposed necessity.

Damian and I were fortunate to share each Christmas season together. Cindy would travel to Las Vegas to be with her two sons and the grandchildren. I flew Damian down to Florida. Usually, we would do things we both enjoyed, like fishing in the bays of Sarasota, Florida, shooting handguns at an inside range, and creating our own beer-brewery crawls. Of course, one highlight for both of us was our Christmas meal, which would always contain some type of pasta, such as lasagna or fettucine, meatballs, antipasto, and the like in the tradition of Mamie. I had prepared this kind of meal since Damian's birth, so it had become a wonderful tradition for us for over fifty years. Coupled with the Christmas meal, we always went to a specialty restaurant for dinner on Christmas Eve, after which we exchanged gifts.

It was obvious how much Damian enjoyed my efforts, and we always relished a glorious week during which we recalled events we shared in our lives. "Dad, do you remember after the divorce when we went sledding? You were sliding down the hill in a small disk when a small mogul launched you about two feet in the air, and you shouted, 'Oh, shit!'"

I replied, "Yes, I remember that, but I landed *in* the disk, right?" The bantering continued back and forth. We seemed to talk about so many things: politics, his savings and investment strategies, views of religion, what we were each working toward, dreams for the future, challenges currently in our lives, some of my "vandalism" escapades, and so on. The list was endless. The intimacy was priceless.

In summary, I could not have been prouder of a son. Damian's compassion, empathy, altruism, and love were genuine and deep. His accomplishments, both work and personal, were exemplary and healthy. He continued to expand his knowledge and skill sets. We both knew that we were available for each other no matter what might be going on in our respective lives and at any time of the day or night. Our love was total and unconditional. Damian was a unique person and the best son a father could ever hope to have.

Cindy and I sold the Lawrence house after living there for about five years and bought a rustic, largely log-cabin-type house on a private lake south of Indianapolis in Martinsville. The house was posited on top of a hill that gently sloped down to the lake, where we moored our pontoon boat. The boat comfortably accommodated Bailey, Java, any guests visiting, Cindy, and me. The lake was entirely spring-fed and surrounded by old, magnificent hardwood trees that displayed their brilliance and variety in the fall.

Ashley's twins, who were age five or so at the time, would come for weekend visits. Cindy would prepare bubble baths for the "Twinkies," and she would allow them to play and splash to their hearts' content. The focus was on having fun, and flinging bubbles everywhere was simply part of that activity. Cindy would also have cookie-baking sessions with them. To magnify their experience, she made custom chefs' outfits for each, and those outfits were complete with chefs' hats, like the Pillsbury Doughboy, and cooking aprons, adorned with open pockets and replete with age-appropriate rolling pins and other utensils. Beyond the joy and laughter of such moments, we noticed the twins lacked self-confidence. They would not go down a child's slide and displayed no interest in being on swings. They were hesitant, even frightful, to take walks with us through the woods around our house. It was obvious they had been smothered and lacked any self-confidence, and the beautiful and natural setting of our lake house made no difference. For Cindy and me, the entire setting was ideal for summer entertaining and the source of many positive memories.

Among the reasons for moving to Martinsville was to escape the drama that was in full display with Ashley with her manic depression blooming. At the time of this move, Ashley was in the process of truncating vital relationships the twins had with their paternal and maternal grandparents, the twins' father, and seemingly any relationship that could have been beneficial and healthy to their formative years. This was a pattern Ashley demonstrated after each of her three divorces.

Cindy and I also had purchased a Key West–style condominium on Siesta Key, Florida, which served as a great vacation destination and which provided income, as we rented it out most of the year when we were not using it ourselves. In addition, Ricky had had a second home on Siesta Key for decades. It was largely the experiences at that condominium that triggered Cindy asking me one day while we were enjoying a cocktail on the wrap-around deck at the lake house if I would ever consider moving to Florida. I had never thought about it, as I had lived my entire life in Indiana, as opposed to Cindy living in Texas, Virginia, Connecticut, St. Croix, Peru, and so forth. Additionally, I was concerned about being able to continue generating income, servicing my clients, and building assets for retirement. As we would vacation at the condominium, we began to explore more permanent living arrangements in Sarasota County. As fate would have it, during this time, both Bailey and Java passed. The grief and sadness were nearly overwhelming. I knew how important in particular Bailey had been to Cindy, and I tried to be present emotionally and otherwise for her.

Yet, with the passing of Bailey and Java, it suddenly became clear that moving from Indiana to Florida would be much easier, and I had assessed that, with a telephone and computer, I could continue to work and service my clientele, thereby generating income. Furthermore, I no longer had any managerial responsibilities, as I had been fired a *second* time as a general agent for an insurance company. The regional manager apparently did not like that I dressed casually and that I did not have the need to have an official office space, since I worked out of my house. Furthermore, those producers affiliated with me had their own independent office spaces. The whole event was highly disruptive, emotionally and financially, since my termination was out of the blue and abruptly announced at the start of a Monday morning coffee meeting.

Once again, I would be forced to build my personal business back up again. Even though I kept my promises in writing to the regional manager in terms of hiring new associates and production goals, I was not given a grace period or any other choice. In addition, I lost matching on my 401(k) program as well as subsidized health insurance. I worked as an independent contractor in the role of the securities compliance officer for about two years with the new successor manager who was inexperienced and inept and lacked principals. He never recruited, didn't provide training to anyone, and his personal sales production was meager at best. The circumstances made the allure of moving to Florida more appealing. **Positive lessons are learned from negative occurrences or conditions.**

As an aside, the amount of unprofessionalism and outright incompetency in both the insurance and securities industries was alarming, even frightful. So many people were ill-advised, bought horrible products, wasted thousands and thousands of dollars in both commissions and hidden fees, and often received incomplete and poor advice, resulting in lackluster decisions. In any industry, though, there is always room for someone who values education, integrity, service, and places their clients' best interests first. My long-held benchmarks were to be well educated so I could offer sound advice across multiple disciplines, such as insurance, investments, income tax, and estate planning. Secondly, I tried to differentiate myself by superlative service. My standard was to return telephone calls within the same day of receipt. Eventually, my response time was narrowed down to less than one hour. Lastly, I would only recommend products to clients based on my knowledge and if I would have bought those products, too, if in the client's situation.

Cindy and I had contracted to build a new home in Venice, Florida. In July, Cindy would move first and proceed to decorate, make all the window coverings, accommodate furniture arrivals, and set up the house in general. I would commute every six weeks or so by air with the clear goal, when most appropriate, of moving to Florida, too. Our target date for my move was six months later, in December, which allowed me time to see all of my clients, inform them of my ultimate move, and reassure them my service would remain the same. I rented a one-bedroom studio apartment for those six months or so in Greenwood, Indiana, from which I commuted a half hour each way to and from Carmel, Indiana, for my securities and compliance duties. Most of my possessions were in Florida, but I had my desktop computer, golf clubs, and adequate clothing. These arrangements were truly Spartan, but I didn't mind at all, because the goal was so exciting.

Ashley with Walker

Damian and Ken fishing

Ken and Cindy's wedding photo with all four children

Ken and Cindy in Florida

Ken and Cindy on their boat

Dolce Far Niente

Florida, Finnegan, and Cindy

During my penultimate commute to Florida in early November 2013, Cindy asked if I would be willing to meet a rescued dog named Finnegan. We both knew if I agreed to the meeting, the adoption would be completed. Finnegan had lived his first year in complete neglect on a large property where a husband and wife allegedly were caring for a couple *hundred* dogs and cats. The homestead had been raided, and the animals were seized and then distributed to a variety of rescue arrangements. Besides infections, fleas, and the like, Finnegan had a couple of chipped lower front teeth as a result of trying to chew his way out of a cage. He also had a broken tail. Immediately prior to our meeting Finnegan, he had lived with his youthful foster parents and their two dogs for about one year. The foster parents brought Finnegan to our Venice house the day before I headed back to Indiana. Finnegan was predominantly Staffordshire terrier with some shih tzu and whippet, which accounted for his gray with some tan coloring, body shape, and athleticism. His kindness, playfulness, and willingness to please were simply God-given traits.

Finnegan obviously was impacted by the immense trauma of his first year of life. In my absence, Cindy worked with him *daily* and was able to bring him out of his shell, and orient him to trust and love, and understand boundaries. Finnegan embodied perhaps the best characteristics of all of our previous dogs: athleticism, incredible heart, loyalty, willingness to please, deep companionship, and unqualified love.

Of course, he had his own unique mannerisms. A favorite of mine was how he sauntered off to bed after his last urination before night-night. It was a truly unique pattern of a kind of slumbering sleep-walk or mosey. Another favorite mannerism was Finnegan's reaction when I said in an inflated tone, "Mister, what are you dooooooing?" That phrase always triggered Finnegan tilting his head with its fauxhawk patch, with ears at attention and the tips falling over, and with his bottom teeth poking through his curled right lip. Finnegan would look at me with complete focus with his dark eyes protruding from his gray face accentuated by his mini-beard. He looked somewhat like Tramp, had incredible eye contact, and was simply a pure joy on a daily basis. Finnegan lived with us for many years, and our lives would not have been the same without him. He was truly a gift for which we were both grateful on a daily basis.

Our first house in Venice, Florida, opened our eyes to another lifestyle. Temperatures allowed us the freedom to do what we wanted 365 days each year. Given Cindy's adventurous nature, we explored many of the parks for both humans and dogs, restaurants, breweries, community events, farmers' markets, and nearby towns. We also established friendships within the Sawgrass neighborhood and were relatively busy with social gatherings. Ultimately, we became particularly close with two couples. The girls established an annual girls' trip where they traveled to a nearby town in Florida and typically spent a weekend, during which they enjoyed each other's company, wining and dining, soaking up some sun on a local beach, and simply doing things that girls do without husbands' interference, prying, or presence.

That first house in Venice was located on the fourth tee of a semiprivate, twenty-seven-hole golf course. This fueled the rebirth of my playing golf. In the late afternoon, Cindy, Finnegan, and I would walk down the fairway to the fourth hole and rummage in the bushes to find lost golf balls. Needless to say, I did not have to buy a golf ball for ten years. Even more enjoyable, when I played golf, Cindy and Finnegan would join me at the fourth tee. Finnegan sat between Cindy and me in the golf cart. The golf itself was not my focus, although at the time I proudly maintained a four handicap at the age of sixty-seven. Having Cindy and Finnegan ride along with me was what was paramount. Finnegan loved the sights and smells, and Cindy and I simply enjoyed being outside together. We all loved that activity, and when we subsequently moved, we realized how much we had treasured those outings.

Nearly five years later, Cindy came home one afternoon and said, "You won't believe this empty lot I found in Osprey; it's right on Little Sarasota Bay!" Osprey was a small town approximately nine miles north of Venice and two miles south of Sarasota. The location was tranquil and in a small neighborhood much closer to many of the activities that a city the size of Sarasota had to offer.

My initial reaction was to wonder how much that lot cost. It was directly on the water, large, and seemingly was prohibitively expensive. After some brief research, we discovered the lot literally had just gone on the market and was owned by a builder who intended to construct his personal house there. However, the contractor's wife wanted to move back home to England, from which they had departed twenty years earlier, and she felt that having given her husband twenty years in Florida had been sufficient. Therefore, the list price was substantially below market value. The builder and his wife wanted to move the land quickly and go home to England, and we wanted the lot!

I quickly calculated some numbers and conveyed to Cindy that we might be able to buy the lot and build a home on it. She was so excited but cautioned me not to get her hopes up unless there were a valid, realistic basis to do so. It had been my investment modus operandi to fashion client portfolios, including my own, with a *hull* full of stocks of well-diversified blue-chip companies and mutual funds. To that hull, for those who had the inclination, I would add a *jib sail* of higher-risk stocks, predominantly in biotechnology.

In our situation, I had invested heavily in one particular biotech stock by purchasing 100,000 shares at $3.50 per share, since I always had believed in the product's science and the results from each advancing clinical trial. Furthermore, predominantly at Cindy's urging, we margined or borrowed against that account to raise the money for the down payment on the lot, which allowed us to continue owning all of our shares. After a few months, the stock price had fallen to a point that we were within two cents of a margin call, which would have forced us to sell shares of stock and would have cast a dark cloud over our house project on the bay. However, that company eventually was purchased by Gilead at $88 per share, which, needless to say, suddenly brought us a financial independence we never imagined.

Cindy largely designed our Osprey home, and we contracted to build with Legacy Builders, which, after one year, had only poured the foundation. We fired that builder, who subsequently placed a lien on our property for the sole purposes of strong-arming us and "tying us up." My ire was raised to new heights because the lien was clearly fraudulent, and this was a direct attack on home and hearth.

Three years and $100,000 in legal fees later, the judge ruled the lien fraudulent and awarded us attorney fees, court costs, and the like. Of course, collecting the money was another challenge. I never recalled meeting two people who were more malevolent, dishonest, and inimical than the building team, Mike and Wendy Greig, of Legacy Builders.

I reflected on the Cowboy and Mr. Cook telling me I was too naïve and that not everybody operated with the same integrity and transparency as I. This was clearly an example of my not remembering those admonitions and observations. In many circumstances, the ordeal would have crimped many marriages, but Cindy and I were not in one of those. She supported my diligence, at times obsession, in gathering facts, doing research, compiling spreadsheets, and other related activities. In the end, we were victorious, and the dream of a house on the bay became a reality.

After the completion of our house on the bay, Cindy made the house our home. She designed the house in its entirety in detail and selected all of the finishings, such as tile, wallpaper, paint colors, plumbing, and lighting fixtures. I warmly remembered her asking my thoughts and choices on a variety of items. Cindy would present me three examples and ask which I preferred without suggesting her preferences. In *every* instance, my choice was the same as hers. Yes, we were not only compatible but synchronous. More impressively, Cindy made all of the window coverings herself, including nearly ten-foot-high draperies, Roman shades, pillows, seat cushions, and the like. Everything was tied together. Her abilities with color and fabrics were unique and impressive. I periodically wondered how her life may have been different had her natural talents in design been fostered and supported in her youth.

Finnegan

Ken and Cindy moving to Florida

Platinum Years

Similarly to setting up our new home, Cindy also helped guide me into retirement. I received a call out of the blue from a West Palm Beach financial group inquiring what my plans were concerning my *book*, which meant selling my practice as measured by assets under management (AUM) and in-force insurance policies. The group constructed a proposal which was larger in price than I had imagined, and Cindy and I met the principal members of the group for dinner. Following that dinner, I seriously considered executing a contract to sell my practice.

Serendipitously, the day after dinner, as I was mulling the decision with Cindy to sell my practice, I received a call from a former advanced sales manager and friend of mine, Tim Reidy. He, too, inquired about my retirement thoughts, and I conveyed the pending proposal. Tim and another former branch manager of mine from northeastern Indiana, Bill Pendleton, fashioned a similar proposal.

At that time, I had known both Tim and Bill for more than twenty years, had worked with them in the field with clients, and knew their integrity, attention to detail, and focus on their clients rather than personal gain. Besides our former business relationship, Tim and I were friends. We respected each other and had sought each other's opinions and feedback on a number of both personal and business issues over the years. In short order, the sale was consummated!

The annual payments were more than enough to meet my needs for each of the following five years. Furthermore, ninety-five percent of the payments were characterized as long-term capital gains, which significantly softened the income tax consequences of the annual buy-out payments. We executed the paperwork with the understanding that it was critically important to me that my clients of forty-plus years would receive high-quality counseling in a transparent way with a particular focus on timely service. Those parameters were far more important than the money involved.

Early retirement was not too difficult for me, although it is seemingly so for men in general. Some men of my generation, as it seemed to me, were accustomed to being hunters and gatherers, or providers, if you will. To most responsible men, hunting and gathering was a caretaking function. Suddenly, that function, and whatever it might mean to one's self-worth, was absent in my life. Yet, selling my practice was not particularly bothersome for me since I had mentally and emotionally decided I was ready to retire, and the buyout of the biotech stock had created a huge boost to the net worth of many of my clients.

It was appropriate timing to retire on a high note. Retirement to me did not equate to stopping all other activities. In fact, I had more time to do whatever I chose. In addition, I had committed to Tim and Bill that I would be available and involved somewhat at a distance. Clients still called for my input and reactions to proposals, though much less time was involved than before since I had given my blessing to the new partners. As one business owner remarked, "Ken, you have been with me longer than my husband, so I hope you don't mind if I call *you* from time to time." Of course, I didn't mind. I was rather flattered, and those attestations reinforced that my professionalism, abilities, and service model had indeed been of value to clients.

I suddenly had a lot of time on my hands. In the early days, I used some of that time for extra walks with Finnegan and increased dinners out with Cindy. Thankfully, I could afford to do whatever I wanted, and there were infinite possibilities. Cindy and I increased our travel, particularly to Europe, and I began playing some golf after a three-year hiatus. Most importantly, I had time to collect my thoughts in writing about my memories. Initially, memorializing my memories was for the purpose of a gift to my son, Damian, and to any grandchildren who might someday be predisposed to learning more about Papi. Moreover, the grander intent was that, with assistance and potential restructuring, my memories might be published, thereby fulfilling an aspiration that someone would read my memories and see that, out of somewhat dire and at times potentially debilitating circumstances, a person can rise to success on multiple levels, financial and personal. Beyond all of this, Cindy and I were able to choose what we wanted to do, where we wanted to travel, and how we wanted to enjoy our lives together. That freedom and ability, coupled with both of us enjoying good health, was truly a blessing.

Being married to Cindy was beyond description because she was so multifaceted beyond her personal, admirable characteristics. For example, Cindy also loved food and cooking, and it was as if a gourmet meal of sorts was more normal than not on a daily basis. After seventeen years of marriage, my physique is a testimony to her abilities and a cause for my renewed, though disliked, working out some each day. Thankfully, I was able to lose some weight, and I did feel better. As I aged, maintaining a reasonable weight required a certain degree of vigilance. I was reminded nearly weekly that life was finite as I observed friends and acquaintances passing. Since working out and monitoring my volume of food intake intuitively translated to living a couple more years of such a wonderful life, I seized the opportunity.

Cindy and I were also fortunate to develop strong interests in ethnic food, craft beers, and wine. Our local area, perhaps not different from other ones, was peppered with craft breweries. Additionally, we were able to travel more extensively and beyond our dreams from anytime previous in our lives. We averaged going to Europe twice *each* year and largely traversed all the major European rivers and Europe as a whole. Among the well-known cities were Paris, Rome, Venice, Athens, Bordeaux, Lisbon, and Barcelona. There were also countless small towns and even villages throughout Germany, France, Belgium, Switzerland, Italy, Greece, Portugal, and Spain.

Of course, on those adventures, we immersed ourselves as best we could in the local culture in terms of food and drink as well as the historical sights. Cindy's fluency in Spanish and related interest in other languages in general allowed her to find spots frequented by locals throughout Europe, particularly in Spain, France, Italy, and Germany. Cindy simply loved languages, especially when she was challenged to use her skills in practice. In summary, we were blessed to have each other and to have shared, genuine interests coupled with the ability to explore them more extensively.

Cindy has tremendous creativity and superlative skills in many areas of home and hearth in addition to cooking: décor, design, and sewing, to name a few. Yet, what makes Cindy unique is a combination of characteristics and the depth of those characteristics. Perhaps, like me, her first marriage to the father of her two sons may have been to an *idea* rather than to a more rational set of facts and basic compatibility. This is not to say that Cindy didn't love her husband, but her innate desires to travel, to explore, and to grow, as well as her desire to have children, weren't present in that husband. In fact, the first son was fashioned around a quid pro quo that if Cindy could have a baby, the father would get a Corvette. After Cindy's subsequent divorce from her sons' father, he never gave Cindy a penny toward raising the boys, and the idea of even contributing, let alone encouraging attendance, to college was an alien concept to him. Even as the boys matured, he paid little to no attention to either boy and never made a sincere effort to know them or be part of their lives, let alone two grandchildren in Las Vegas, a short distance, in relative terms, from El Paso, Texas. Cindy and I shared the experience of having been married to someone who took little to no genuine interest in the children. That commonality was another layer of mortar binding us together.

On the other hand, Cindy wanted everything for her boys. That desire, I believe, was the source of her entering into a couple of relationships prior to our meeting. Namely, she was focused on the *idea* of a whole family, complete with activities like camping and the tutelage of a male father figure to her boys. Regardless, no matter the conditions, Cindy made sure her boys were clothed and fed and had a clean home in which to live. It didn't matter how much work she had to do; it didn't matter if that meant she had to work at three jobs at the same time. Cindy became a master of frugality. Cindy gave all of herself for the welfare of her two boys and similarly to Bailey and Java, too. In short, she was responsible for and loved her boys and did whatever was required. Her selflessness and dedication were among her most admirable qualities. Damian loved Cindy, felt very close to her, and was appreciative of her taking care of Dad. Our attitudes and responsibilities for our children were yet another layer of mortar binding us together.

To have provided food, clothing, and shelter by herself was admirable, yet to do such couched in accountability was exceptional. Regarding accountability, while on St. Croix, Cindy had managed to get her sons jobs. One job for Jesse was at a high-end, well-established restaurant when he was seventeen or eighteen years old. Sometime later, a couple of friends from Texas came for a visit, and Jesse chose to stay home and carouse with his visiting friends. After the discovery of her son abandoning the job at the restaurant, Cindy ultimately told Jesse she would buy him a one-way ticket to anywhere in the United States because he wasn't going to stay on the island, not work, and sit around. That accountability was remarkable, took strength, and was a great learning experience. Jesse always concurred that his mother's purchase of a one-way ticket was important to his self-development and maturation, and it was the correct decision to have been rendered. This was not to say that Cindy didn't value or abrogated the health and well-being of her two sons. On the contrary, her dedication and love for her two sons is unmatched and unconditional. No other person, including me, is more important or even equal in her eyes than her two sons. I have always admired, even revered, Cindy's devotion as a mother.

I periodically reflect on watching the musical *Camelot* on television as a youth and the tremendous impact that viewing had on me. In particular, the song "How to Handle a Woman" was uniquely penetrating. In my earlier life, I dreamt about a life with a wife to whom I would give all that I could, and that love and respect would be reflected back on me. In Cindy, I was blessed to find such. I try to tell Cindy daily that I love her. I also attempt to reflect my love and devotion to Cindy through my actions. My actions include something as simple as bringing her coffee in bed every morning while she is waking up or as large as surprising her after sixteen years of marriage with a new, large diamond for a restructured wedding ring she could design. What I attempt to do is "love her, love her, simply love her." I am thankful each morning when I wake up to having Cindy next to me and in my life. **Love is the most powerful energy.**

Water has always been a source of wonderment for me and an inducement to thinking and reflection. I have always had choices. The choices I made throughout my life brought me to this point with Cindy. I flourished despite all the obstacles I had to overcome. So, with Cindy, my life evolved as a metamorphic and karmic circle. It began with an alcoholic mother whose attention was focused on herself in a disjointed and destructive or inimical manner to ultimately having a true partner in Cindy in a relationship of transparency, respect, and love.

It was a journey filled with challenges that required my development of a variety of skills and choices. That journey also molded my character and fashioned my life's lessons. Yet, I never thought that my journey was singular in nature. That is, I believed other people had their own journeys full of challenges, choices, and actions. My hope is that the reader of the memories of my life's journey can identify moments to which you can relate and ponder the choices I made. In so doing, you can extract what may have been illustrative or instructive and discard the rest. I have always believed and felt that I am very blessed and fortunate. I truly always have been. I am so fully aware of the many blessings in spite of momentary confrontations. All of the challenges, trials, and tribulations made me who I am. I am proud, thankful, humble, and blessed.

Sunset at home

Lessons Learned

Upon reflecting on some memories, I identified personal character-istics and behaviors that served me exceedingly well for the most part. As I learned, actions are far more important than my words or thoughts. Behaviors are actions. I thought it important to add some detail, context, and color to some of my life's lessons and resulting behaviors from my memories.

(1.) If something is worth doing, **do it now**. This behavior prevented, after a few days, weeks, or even months, the creation of a list of *many* things to do, which tended to contribute to further procrastination because the length of the list would appear overwhelming. Without the completion of tasks, my mind was continuously drawn to what needed to be done. Worrying and thinking about what needed to be done was a waste of energy and time. Time was my most valuable commodity: It could not be duplicated or manufactured. For all of us, time is finite. As I aged, time became increasingly valued. From a client's per-spective, the get-it-done-now feature separated me from many other advisors. More than once I heard from clients, "I wish that so-and-so would act as quickly as you do. I know things get done, and I don't have to follow up."

Yet, I exhibited the do-it-now behavior to extremes sometimes. Cindy teased me, for example, that I vacated the dinner table to do the dishes too quickly, but my impulse was to wash the dishes immediately so I would have more time to spend leisurely with her. Just because I thought that way didn't make it right. I was simply oriented to doing something as soon as circumstances permitted. It was true, though, that I was inclined to obsess about doing things immediately, and this was something I needed to work on in terms of balance.

(2.) Closely related to "do-it-now" was my attitude that if something were worth doing, then to **do it right the first time**. This may have seemed obvious on its face, but having to *redo* something results in wasting time, that precious commodity, and often with greater expense. It also creates the possibility of being added to the proverbial to-do list discussed above. I also knew in the past that when I took a shortcut, I would think about it for days, maybe even obsess a bit, until I went back to the task and did it right. The entire process of having to go back and fix something is couched in negative energy, wasted time, and additional expense.

(3.) **Impulsivity** was my friend at times and also my foe in other instances, so I needed to be on guard and vigilant. On the one hand, impulsive responses tied into my get-it-done-now inclination. Tasks were completed, and to-do lists were minimized. However, impulsivity at times caused me to overindulge or overreact too quickly, and those occurrences were not typically healthy or sound. Impulsivity in my life also resulted in unhealthy and troubling relationships with others. Jodi and Jeanine were two clear examples. Too often, my impulsivity caused me to go rabbit hunting with a nuclear warhead or to be too generous too quickly. In being vigilant, it was critical that I identify more objectively the person toward whom my impulsivity was directed. Additionally, it was important that I more logically assess a person and thereby apply the correlative degree and speed of my actions. I learned moderation, as in the song "Question of Balance" by the Moody Blues, but impulsivity was another area where I needed to spend time and focus.

(4.) **The mind is my most powerful organ.** I had a choice in what to think, and I had the ability to manifest what I thought. This was not some kind of hocus pocus; many positive and productive outcomes happened. Too often, I believed people underestimated and underutilized their minds. My brain was trained or exercised just like any other muscle group: It was my choice of growth instead of atrophy. Meditation was invaluable. Completing word puzzles or math challenges on a daily basis for even a few minutes was productive.

From the *Brihadaranyaka Upanishad*: "You are what your deep driving desire is. As your desire is, so is your will. As your will is, so is your deed. As your deed is, so is your destiny."

(5.) **Organization is powerful.** My propensity for organization probably was developed, or at least considerably heightened, during my first marriage. Building a practice on straight commission, being my children's chauffeur to and from school, and coaching or attending all athletic activities, cleaning, cooking, and performing what house maintenance I could, necessitated that I become organized. Otherwise, things simply would not get completed. Some of those items were not optional. Making a living and taking care of the kids required I become highly efficient, which required being organized. On a simpler level, I tracked personal expenses month by month on an annual basis in an Excel spreadsheet. As a result, I was able to easily reference prior-year expenditures for things like car or homeowner's insurance and readily know if the renewal premiums were in line or exorbitant. It saved me time in researching, and it saved me money. It also identified how much money I needed to make. The saved time allowed me to complete other tasks.

(6.) **Don't be afraid to get help.** I certainly never believed I knew or could do everything. I never had a clue about how an engine worked when I looked under the hood of my car. I was not aware of the most recent changes or finer details in estate or income tax laws. If I had to anchor something into drywall, there was a likelihood that it would not happen and I was left with a large hole. If I paid for advice from an attorney, for example, I accepted the advice and acted accordingly. If I needed help processing events or emotional troubles, I sought the advice of a therapist. I would have wasted time and money seeking, obtaining, and paying for advice if I didn't follow that counsel. Listening was one thing; taking action on the advice was most important.

Early in my life, I did not ask others for their opinion or for guidance. It likely was due to my low self-esteem and feelings of inadequacy or shame. As I matured, I found asking others for their advice or opinion was not only advisable but also valuable. The Cowboy always delivered his opinion or advice in an unvarnished fashion. If his advice were counter to my thoughts, he would delicately say, "Dago, just chew on it." Seeking advice and opinions from others was a positive reflection of self-worth for me, and I benefitted immensely.

(7.) I learned more from negative occurrences or even disappointments than from positive ones. Sometimes, as was the case with my mother, I learned from her example whom I didn't want to be or how I didn't want to act. I had an early image fostered by my father of how I wanted to treat people and how I hoped I would be viewed by them. **Positive lessons are learned from negative occurrences or conditions.** My mother's *example* in particular taught me to be empathetic with people.

(8.) **Don't judge a book by its cover.** I recall having lunch with a good friend and client, my veterinarian of possum fame. During lunch, I told Roger I was getting a divorce from Jodi. He couldn't believe it; he said we always *looked* like the perfect couple. Little did Roger know of the constant trials and tribulations within the walls of our house and well beyond raccoons and opossums. Equally superficially, I could have judged little Joey as not being a good baseball player because he was missing an arm, but he became an all-star and was an example and inspiration to all of us. Simply, I could not know what it was like to walk in the shoes of someone else; I could not know what challenges and conditions they faced or with which they currently struggled. It was always superior to seek first to understand, then be understood. It served me far better to not judge.

I attempted to take time to employ patience when evaluating situations as they may not be what they appeared at first blush. I often told the salesmen I trained that it was critical that their prospects understood first that the salesperson *cared* before impressing upon the prospective client how much the salesperson might know.

Similarly, if someone viewed the back of my right hand, they would have seen a few scars, some hair, a sunspot, knuckles, and so forth. However, if that same person observed the palm side of the *same* hand, they saw something entirely different: lines, a few callouses, and some wrinkles. It was the same hand, but looking at the palm or the outside of the hand presented two different sets of observations. I tried to see things from **different perspectives**; it allowed empathy to manifest and judgment to restrain. I always had choices in how to view things.

Kahlil Gibran, *The Prophet*: "Your joy is your sorrow unmasked. And the selfsame well from which your laughter rises was oftentimes filled with your tears."

(9.) **Actions speak louder than words.** Thank you, Mr. Cook, Joan, and Cowboy. I wish I had absorbed more fully this idiom earlier in life, but I am thankful to have finally understood it. When I listened to politicians, I was reminded repeatedly of how empty and misleading words by themselves were. I used to hear, few though they were, nice words and statements of affection from Jodi and from my mother. Yet, an objective bystander would simultaneously have seen their *actions* toward me, and those actions in no way, shape, or form supported the words. Their actions, in reality, obliterated their words and more accurately reflected their true feelings either about me or, more likely, was a projection about themselves. Either way, it was not healthy, let alone loving. If I relied on observing actions over time, I made more realistic, rational, and likely accurate judgments about people.

(10.) As the Cowboy once told me, **"It's okay that you are number one to you sometimes."** To be the best I could be for others, it was critical that I periodically indulged in myself or simply replenished. It was always superior to take time to sharpen the saw. It would cut more easily if I did so. I accomplished this in a variety of ways and in simple terms; the methods and activities were not time consuming, expensive, or excessive. Meditation was one such example.

There were times when I could not do what another asked, and that was okay. There were times when a relationship felt toxic. If actions clearly reflected such toxicity, it was okay to minimize contact or, if need be, to terminate the relationship. For me, those terminated relationships always entailed aspects of Mr. Cook's/ Joan's prescriptive observation of people with behaviors lacking empathy, being all talk, operating without any reciprocity, etc. It was appropriate, even healthy, to remove such relationships from my life, thereby leaving a healthier and better "me" for others.

(11.) It has always been important to me to **act consistent with my true self**. I believe I have always been a kind and compassionate person, and I was never sorry or regretful for acting that way. I recall when going through my divorce, I was at the checkout counter at a Walmart during Christmas season. A young girl and her mother were in front of me, and the little girl was holding two dolls. The young girl asked the cashier how much the dolls cost. Her mother said to her daughter, "Yes, they are beautiful, but you know we can't afford those. I'm sorry." I caught the eye of the checkout lady and gestured that I would pay for the two dolls *and* the groceries in their cart. I really didn't have that much money at that time due to the divorce proceedings, but I had a credit card. The look on the little girl's face was forever etched in my mind and heart. Indeed, it was I who received the gift by acting consistent with my "true" self.

Act 1, Scene 3 of Shakespeare's *Hamlet*: "To thine own self be true, and it must follow, as the night the day. Thou canst not then be false to any man."

(12.) **My actions and relationships do matter.** I believe that I always tried to leave the campsite better than I found it. I believe this was true of relationships and even routine behavior around people who, for the most part, were strangers. It costs nothing to be kind, compassionate, and helpful. As I look back on my life, those moments from which I derived the greatest joy, pleasure, and fulfillment always involved a relationship, be it with a canine companion or, more importantly, Cindy, Damian, and my closest friends. I have never thought nor heard a client who asked me to come to his side in his final hours say, "Ken, I wish I had worked more." That certainly was not what Donna said to me. Having felt that relationships are so important, I maintain they deserve more attention than work or leisure. What is of paramount importance are my relationships, and I am truly blessed in my relationships, both personal and business.

(13.) While it may not have appeared so around the time of my divorce, Deepak Chopra told me, **"Everything is exactly as it should be in the moment, and there are infinite possibilities."** This concept was exceedingly challenging at times, even beyond comprehension. Following my divorce, I had, among others, two fundamental choices. One, I could have wallowed in self-pity and been consumed with the emotional, psychological, and financial devastation. I could have indulged in alcohol. On the other hand, I could have chosen an opposite path and, at least *tried* to fashion a new, fulfilling, and healthy life. The aforementioned were simply two choices among infinite possibilities.

The idiom "when one door closes, another opens" seemed universally true in my life, as long as I remain open to the possibilities. When I am troubled by an event or a person, my self-talk progresses through a series of questions and analyses, which is an activity by which I became somewhat obsessive. What is my role? Could I have seen this coming? What should I do differently?

Once I am satisfied with my *answers*, I typically pivot to the fact that I have myriad choices, and I am best served if I do not operate too impulsively with the first or seemingly *best* answer. Meditation is invaluable in this setting. Ultimately, though, the key is to *take action* because nothing happens with thinking alone. Action is a required step.

Finally, I tend to assess how things are progressing with my course of action and evaluate the apparent consequences. It is a key for me that I remember most things do not happen or manifest on my timeline, and I am best served by a heavy dosage of patience. It is prudent for me to make adjustments along the way. It is always the journey that is most important, not the destination.

As one of my childhood friend's mother's, Nettie, said to me around the time I moved out of my mother's house in high school, "It is not what happens but what one *does* with what happens that is most important." This perspective has multiple benefits. In terms of reacting to, perhaps, an unpleasant circumstance or outcome, this perspective forces a shift in mindset to action as opposed to being spellbound or stuck. This is not to suggest I don't evaluate my role in the immediate circumstance or outcome. My behavior and reactions remain paramount. Once analyzed, I do not default to feelings of blame or inadequacy; rather, I use the circumstance, coupled with a picture of the desired outcome, to manifest growth and a positive orientation.

(14.) **The greatest sin is not to have failed, but to have never tried.** I read versions of this by Tennyson, Churchill, and Edmund Burke. For some reason, it resonates deeply within me. It is true that I won many championships in athletics. It is true that peers elected me to the Board of Financial Service Professionals in Indiana, and that clients voted me as Top Advisor of the Year. It is true that I was published in financial press. It is also true that I was terminated *twice* as a general agent.

On a personal level, it is also true that only one of two children became well-adjusted and exemplary. Likewise, I was successful in one of two marriages. In all cases, I gave all I had with dignity, empathy, and compassion. My conclusion on the personal level is that I batted at a five hundred level, which in major league baseball would have won the batting championship every year. All joking aside, the truth is, in athletics, my career, parenting, and marriage, I had many setbacks and even failures at some level. I learned far more through my failures than my successes.

As I had heard many times, I could not change people, places, or things. Acceptance is a volitional act. So, I may have failed at times; but by never giving up and always trying, I completed a highly successful career, raised an exemplary son, and am married to a woman who is the epitome of my dreams.

(15.) It is simply amazing how much I accomplished when **I coupled inspiration with perspiration and enveloped those features with focus and persistence.** Standing still is not a chosen option at any time. Setbacks are always viewed as temporary and as an indication to focus and then to move in a different direction. I believe that persistence and hard work lead to breakthroughs as conveyed by the Doors in "Break On Through (To the Other Side)." I understand that my timeline does not require matching some preconceived dictum. My inspiration is strongest when I am *acting for the benefit of someone else.* For some clients who were parents, my actions and counsel focused on assuring the financial safety and education of children. For other clients, my actions and focus remained on their objectives, such as the purchase of a second home or manufacturing a comfortable retirement. For Cindy, it simply is consistently manifesting my love of her.

Owning a totally custom home on a bay facing the west—and hence sunsets—is something I had never thought about, probably due to what might have seemed an inordinate amount of money required to build and maintain such. Once Cindy had identified the available lot, my *inspiration* kicked into high gear, and I fashioned all kinds of spreadsheets reflecting investment returns, tax consequences, cash flow, and the like. My persistence in modeling expenditures depending on finishing selections and labor expenses was detailed and reassuring. The inspiration and persistence were for Cindy.

Along the way, the biotech stock exploded, but Cindy and I kept frugality at the forefront without sacrificing choices. The fraudulent lien was ultimately an interruption and distraction. We stayed *focused*, *persistent*, and on course.

Similarly, the mountain of debt after my divorce was simply a bad memory; yet I had taken pride in what I had been able to build in a relatively short time period of twenty years. Our financial situation is all due to inspiration, a lot of *perspiration*, and singular focus and persistence.

Finally, I garner enormous inner peace in the knowledge that, after my likely first passing, Cindy will be more than comfortable no matter how long she lives, and that assets will be protected for her from creditors and not subject to probate or liability claims. When combined, the protection from creditors, the dramatic reduction in probate fees, and the savings in estate transfer taxes allow significant bequests through trust distributions to, among others, Walker, Parker, and Beau, the three grandchildren present in my life.

(16.) **Love is the most powerful energy of all.** No matter the now distant and raw events of my past or the challenges, disappointments, or obstacles in some past moments, love in its mere presence overcame all. Love immediately delivers me to a feeling of "life is good." For me, it is because the dimensions and attributes of love are antithetical to the characteristics of people whom I should avoid. Love is action, empathetic, reciprocal, and intoxicating in and of itself. It forms an incredible foundation of trust and respect, and above all else, is expansive and empowering. It is my firm belief that when I feel love, I touch the Divine, and in those moments, I know God. I believe we all are truly powerful, spiritual beings, as my friend of many years,

Fr. Justin Belitz, often proclaimed. God is present in all of us. It is through *relationships* that love is manifested and expanded.

Furthermore, it is my belief that God is the source of love. From the day long ago in diapers at the water's edge and throughout my life, I have been incredibly blessed with being able to access and hear God's voice and feel His presence. I believe many people did so, too, in that they "had a feeling" or their conscience, that little voice, presented itself in the forefront. I also know that meditation is a powerful tool to *listen* to God, particularly when "coming out" of a session. When I am overcome with intense feelings of love in a moment, I believe I am experiencing the Divine and feeling His presence.

Finally, my experiences of love are continuous, full, and pure, particularly with Damian and Cindy and on a different level with my canine companions. Yes, it is true that Cindy and I have basic compatibility, a key component, as the Cowboy, Joan, and Mr. Cook all conveyed. Yet, our relationship extends beyond compatibility to fluidity and synchronicity. Cindy and I share values and general orientations. We so often, almost daily, make comments about which the other person would instantly say, "I was just thinking that very same thing." Indeed, we are in tune with one another.

I am thankful every morning at 6:30 when I take Finnegan on a walk because I recognize someday that those walks will not be available. Carpe diem!

I am thankful that Damian always performs his welfare check, as he labels his telephone calls to me, sometime during each week. Damian is always present.

I am thankful *every* morning when I awaken that Cindy is by my side and in my life.

Damian

Damian and Finnegan

Parting Thoughts about Myself

Throughout my life, if I describe consistent facets of my personality, I use attributes of compassion, kindness, generosity, empathy, tenacity, intelligence, and competition. I also add tones of being obsessive, impatient, and emotive. As is likely true for all of us, how people in our lives see us may be similar in some respects and dissimilar in others from self-perception. It is not a matter of who is right. More importantly, the entirety of the commentaries likely blend to form an accurate mosaic of our authentic selves. I asked those who knew me the longest and closest to describe me from their perspectives.

Jerry conveyed, "It's so hard to condense our relationship into a few words after forty-plus years. I'm not sure I have ever met anyone like you in my life. I'm proud to call you my friend, business associate, mentor, and confidant. These words/things came to mind when I thought about you: honesty, integrity, common sense, generosity, kindness, trustworthiness, considerate. To just sum it all up, you're a damn good human that I'm proud to call my friend. Luv ya, my brother from another mother!"

My consistent friend of seventy-plus years, Ricky, conveyed that I was trustworthy, conscientious, loyal, communicative, bright, athletic, tenacious, and his best friend for life.

It was interesting to note that my son, Damian, viewed me as kind, compassionate, empathetic, selfless, tenacious, driven, analytical, and true to self.

Cindy articulated that I was romantic, generous, considerate, athletic, competitive, and frugal as well as impatient and hypersensitive.

I am pleased that those closest to me possess largely congruent views and positively reflect the kind of person I aspired to be. I always thought that if friends were meaningful, they should take priority in terms of my time and efforts. Friends are more important than work or any leisure activity, so it seems to me they were the best investment I could ever make. I am thankful and feel blessed in the number and quality of friends in my life. Relationships do matter.

In reading some of my memories and reflecting on my commentary about them, it is my fervent hope that some of your own memories, thoughts, and feelings were triggered. I do not assume that my challenges were particularly unique, severe, or unfortunate. Rather, I am hopeful that how I responded and characteristics I developed as a direct result of my experiences would be thought-provoking for you and, in some cases, suggestive of hope. To me, my life is all about choices, consequences of choices, and *taking action with love* for one's self and others.

In any case, from my heart to yours with love, be well!

Ken